SUMMA PUBLICATIONS, INC.

Thomas M. Hines
Publisher

William C. Carter
Editor-in-chief

Editorial Board

William Berg
University of Wisconsin

Germaine Brée
Wake Forest University

Michael Cartwright
McGill University

Hugh M. Davidson
University of Virginia

Elyane Dezon-Jones
Washington University

John D. Erickson
Louisiana State University

Wallace Fowlie (emeritus)
Duke University

James Hamilton
University of Cincinnati

Freeman G. Henry
University of South Carolina

Norris J. Lacy
Washington University

Jerry C. Nash
University of New Orleans

Allan Pasco
University of Kansas

Albert Sonnenfeld
University of Southern California

Orders:
Box 20725
Birmingham, AL 35216

Editorial Address:
3601 Westbury Road
Birmingham, AL 35223

Mothers, Madams, and "Lady-like" Men

Mothers, Madams, and "Lady-like" Men

Proust and the Maternal

Elizabeth Richardson Viti

SUMMA PUBLICATIONS, INC.
Birmingham, Alabama
1994

Copyright 1994
Summa Publications, Inc.
ISBN 1-883479-01-0

Library of Congress Catalog Number 94-69024

Printed in the United States of America

All rights reserved.

Marcel Proust Studies
vol. 4

For my grandmother

Contents

Acknowledgments	ix
Introduction	1
Chapter One Proustian Dichotomy: Good Mothers and Bad (or Where's Papa?)	9
Chapter Two The Proustian Mother and Object Relations Theory	25
Chapter Three Albertine à la Dinnerstein	39
Chapter Four Mothers and Daughters: The Lesbian Continuum	57
Chapter Five "Mommy Dearest"	77
Conclusion	105
Bibliography	111

Acknowledgements

Both personal and institutional support made this project possible. I would like to thank Eugène Nicole and Serge Doubrovsky for their early confidence in me and Margaret Cook and Joan Givner for sustaining that confidence when it was most needed. Nothing compares, however, to the ongoing encouragement of Robert M. Viti. Finally, I am most grateful to the Grants Advisory Commission of Gettysburg College for its financial support.

—*E. R. V.*

Introduction

Time and again I have wondered why there has not been a feminist reading of Marcel Proust's *A la recherche du temps perdu,* particularly because the author is a hero to so many Franco-feminist critics. The moment seems propitious for such a project: not only is feminist criticism flourishing, but also, four new editions of Proust's masterpiece have appeared within the past few years, not to mention Richard Howard's forthcoming translation or Ronald Hayman's recent biography of Proust. Furthermore, the much discussed and controversial sexual ambiguity of the novel's characters, in particular its women, fairly cries out for an interpretation which acknowledges that gender informs and complicates writing (as well as reading). And the overwhelming number of important women in *La Recherche* implies a fascination with femininity which supports the feminist perspective that attitude toward sexual difference can generate and structure a literary text.

Indeed, women, not men, make the novel move. At the very least the great Proustian themes find their best illustration among the female characters: the Salon is a matriarchal domain that allows men a marginal role where, for example, M. Verdurin is La Patronne's assistant, a turn-of-the-century "go-for" whose only value is to make his wife's wish his command. Women most adroitly play the Salon's requisite parlor game, Snobbishness, and out of thin air they create new identities that move them up the social scale and which, because the various personae are based on essentially nothing, they must ardently protect. These metamorphoses superbly visualize the effects of Time yet simultaneously permit women to make of themselves their own creation with the staying power of Art. Odette moves from her music hall identity of Miss Sacripant to her status as the Duc de Guermantes's mistress and, at the same time, appears to be "une rose stérilisée." Women such as the kitchen-bound Françoise transform tasks seemingly unworthy of the word into Art. The three major artists of *La Recherche,* Bergotte, Elstir and Vinteuil, all depend on women in some way to realize their creativity. Finally, Proustian women are, of course, inextricably linked to the theme of Love.

Certainly any justification of women as motivation for Proust's masterpiece must also include the momentous cup of tea, sign of Sunday morning visits to Tante Léonie's room, from which the novel springs. Henceforth, the novel moves along through the important moments of Marcel's life all of which are linked to women, for as Germaine Brée appropriately notes, any period not so marked falls into oblivion (Brée 1967, 204). Moreover, Marcel's epiphanies about time and selfhood are anchored to a female figure: the narrator bends to tie his shoelace and both unexpectedly recalls how his grandmother once lovingly performed this simple task and comes to understand "les intermittences du cœur"; Balbec, its Grand Hôtel and "la petite bande" body forth from a stiff table napkin; and an uneven cobblestone in Venice resuscitates the memory of the narrator's mother. Fittingly Mlle de Saint-Loup closes the novel as the very image of all the narrator's experiences, the meeting of Swann's Way and Guermantes's Way, which is the novel Marcel is about to write.

Critical too is Lisa Appignanesi's study, *Femininity and the Creative Imagination,* which places femininity center stage as the source of Proust's genius. Not only does she examine how femininity is fruitful to the writer's art but also what the myth of femininity reveals about the author's vision and, thirdly, what Proust observes in the myth of femininity which is useful to an understanding of women (157-215). Clearly Appignanesi has no difficulty accepting the female characters as such and is somewhat mystified by those who simultaneously label Proust a "feminine" author and yet find him incapable of portraying women.

But though female critics, interestingly enough, find Proust's women believable, as do certain notable male scholars, Harry Levin and Maurice Bardèche among them, the men-in-women's clothing perspective nonetheless has a long tradition and, in fact, has become a cliché in Proustian scholarship. As early as 1921 Jacques-Emile Blanche addressed the author of *La Recherche* in a preface to *Dates:* "Il me semble parfois . . . que vous empruntiez à un sexe les traits d'un autre; qu'en certaines de vos effigies, il y ait substitution partielle du 'genre', si bien qu'on pourrait dire il au lieu d'elle" (xv-xvi). Subsequently women became the focus of the sexual ambiguity debate when, in the thirties, Robert Vigneron suggested that Proust's chauffeur, Alfred Agostinelli, was the model for Albertine, and thus the writer's women were men in disguise. This theory was fed by Proust's suspected homosexuality and later developed by Justin O'Brien in his well known article "Albertine the Ambiguous: Notes on Proust's Transposition of the Sexes." Most recently J. E. Rivers seems subtly to revive the idea in *Proust and the Art of Love*. He never entirely rejects the O'Brien hypothesis because he joins both O'Brien and Vigneron in their willingness to accept certain biographical information to justify men as the inspiration for fictional women.

Perhaps Rivers does this primarily to support his view, and I would agree, that homosexual relationships can serve as a model for love as easily as heterosexual relationships. Perhaps he does this to underscore the bisexuality of the novel's characters, seeing as he does, in contrast to Appignanesi, androgyny not femininity as Proust's creative inspiration. Whatever the case, the unsatisfying result in this long overdue and otherwise interesting study of homosexuality is to diminish the importance of women in Proust's novel. Discussion of femininity is limited to homosexuals who "derive from their inner, feminine selves a host of talents and abilities which are usually held to be the exclusive province of women" (185) or to Mlle Vinteuil and Albertine, obvious examples of lesbianism, though there is never a satisfactory examination of female inversion.

Eve Kosofsky Sedgwick is less of a disappointment even though, in *Epistemology of the Closet,* she inquires primarily into Euro-American male sexual definition. She is admittedly apologetic: "That limitation seems a damaging one chiefly insofar as it echoes and prolongs an already scandalously extended eclipse: the extent to which women's sexual, specifically homosexual, experience and definition tend to be subsumed by men's during the turn-of-the-century period most focused on in my discussion . . ." (39). Moreover, in her chapter on Proust, while examining primarily *Sodome et Gomorrhe* and Charlus, and only Albertine among the female characters, she, nonetheless, gives some valuable insights into the young woman's sexuality. But bothersome in both studies is the rejection of psychoanalysis. Sedgwick, who has a strong deconstructionist bias, finds it too reductive in its categories of the Mother, the Father, the preoedipal, etc., and Rivers feels that Freud ignores the complexities of everyday life.

In *Psychoanalysis and Feminism* Juliet Mitchell repudiates in particular Rivers's objection, a common one, and cites as an instance of the psychoanalyst's recognition of the social his "Femininity" lecture in which Freud discusses how custom, not simply repressed psychical structures, force women into a passive role. Moreover, she further reproaches Freud's critics by noting that it is equally as *inappropriate to apply standards of reality to the unconscious* (14). But more important here is Mitchell's preoccupation with the relationship between psychoanalysis and feminism because, as Malcolm Bowie notes in his study of Proust, Freud and Lacan, feminist efforts in the area are crucial among the assorted initiatives at present taking place (4). In fact, I could not help but be reminded of these recent undertakings as I read the introduction to Leo Bersani's *Marcel Proust,* which appeared in the sixties. Ironically, Bersani (were he to replace the word men with women) could easily be describing what has occurred in feminist psychoanalytic criticism during the past twenty years: "The men who have engaged in this sort of study by no means form a single school of critical thought; but in spite of considerable philosophical and temperamental differences, they share the wish to describe that level of mental life where the work of art has its origin—the profound and secret impulses that inform the whole work but which the language of the work does not explicitly express" (7).

Currently in feminist circles, literary critics attempting to uncover a text's unconscious intentions represent, on the whole, two divergent perspectives: on the one hand, there is Lacanian theory originating with the late Jacques Lacan's French Freudian School, and on the other hand, there is object relations theory originating with the late British psychoanalyst D. W. Winnicott. The first privileges the Father while the second valorizes the Mother, insisting that all relationships—including literary ones between people and texts—resonate with the profound emotions engendered by and associated with the child's primary caretaker. This second point of view has inspired such seductive texts as Dorothy Dinnerstein's *The Mermaid and the Minotaur* (1976), Nancy Chodorow's *The Reproduction of Mothering* (1978) and numerous books and articles by such literary critics as Marianne Hirsch, Coppelia Kahn, Elizabeth Abel and many others. Furthermore, this theory has the advantage for those of us who are trying to overcome what Domna Stanton aptly calls the Franco-American dis-connection of providing a natural bond to those French feminist thinkers who emphasize the maternal: Hélène Cixous, Julia Kristeva and, most particularly, Luce Irigaray whose texts *L'une ne bouge pas sans l'autre* (1979) and *Le corps-à-corps avec la mère* (1981) are essential in this regard.

However, like Bowie who admittedly hesitates to return to Proust and psychoanalysis, a subject seemingly exhausted, I, too, am reluctant to express interest in Proust and motherhood, a theme ostensibly purged of further meaning. All has been said: the novel finds its genesis in a cup of tea, offered by the narrator's mother-as-muse. The drink's very liquidity suggests femininity and birth, enhanced by an accompanying madeleine which also, Serge Doubrovsky explains in *La Place de la madeleine,* signifies the Mother. Consequently motherhood, not simply redoubled, but tripled, opens *A la recherche du temps perdu* and seems to move the masterpiece through the stages of a pregnancy (Bersani 55). Indeed, Appignanesi sees the Great Mother as the creative symbol of *La Recherche,* and furthermore, Proust himself assumed the identity of a pregnant woman when discussing the creation of the novel (Hayman 293). Biographical information bears witness to the Mother's importance as well. The death of Mme Jeanne Proust is the starting point for all the novelist's best work, for beginning with *Contre Sainte-Beuve,* Proust hoped to resurrect her. Yet, observes Susan Suleiman, the maternal body as body of the text is a notion still capable of renewing our understanding of Proust (357).

I quite agree. For too long readers have simply reacted to the novel's two best known mothers, the narrator's mother and grandmother, and their superiority over all other Proustian women, without defining their differences. Understandably Marcel's attachment to his family members, particularly his mother, is reason enough for their preeminence. However there is a need to move beyond the mother-son relationship and to place the hero's devotion amidst the patterns which emerge after passing other female portraits in review. Part of the feminist critic's task is to plumb the depths of male identification with the Mother and trace its influence on perceptions and depictions of women in general (Kahn 88). This is the appropriate approach to Proust and one which would uncover how the author's preoccupation with and ambivalence toward the Mother unwittingly structures his very definition of femininity, producing everything from bad mothers to surrogate mothers to mothers among men.

Thus, it seems to me fitting and timely to reexamine motherhood in the light of object relations theory which has devoted so much energy to understanding the maternal role. It is time to shift the focus from the Oedipus Complex, an unquestionably significant developmental stage but heretofore synonymous with the mother-son relationship, to the preoedipal where mothers reign supreme. In fact, in the Proustian world fathers are virtually absent, and though many critics explain this absence through an oedipal urge to kill the Father, the secondary role that fathers play in the preoedipal world can justify the paternal vacuum as well. It expresses, it seems to me, an unalleviated bond to the preoedipal mother, a world where everything materializes, not from the Name-of-the-Father, but from the Name-of-the-Mother (Buisine 56).

Moreover, a move to the preoedipal expands analysis from the mother-son relationship solely to the mother-child relationship in general and brings to light how this couple underlies all social order and *all desire* (Irigaray 1981, 14). Indeed, Proust's novel illustrates superbly Dinnerstein's theories which expose adult sexual arrangements for what they are: women and men alike all want to return to Mother. The result is that mothers and daughters prove even more vital to the elaboration of this monumental work. They perversely promote a female power structure which provides the underpinnings of *La Recherche* and announce, through female exclusiveness, the theme of lesbianism, another prominent Proustian preoccupation. Perhaps rivaled in his fascination only by Baudelaire, the novelist offers numerous (documented or suspected) inverted females—Mlle Vinteuil and her companion, Albertine, Andrée, Gilberte, Odette, Mme Verdurin, Rachel, Mme de Guermantes, and the Princesse de Parme among others—who deserve a closer look.

Female homosexuality brings full circle the discussion of sexual ambiguity for it would appear that no longer do men impersonating women people *La Recherche* but rather women *en travesti*. The narrator himself compares the text's homosexual men to girls who disguise themselves as boys in Shakespeare's comedies (III, 23). Of course, biographical information, in particular Proust's own inversion, convinces many readers to see males behind the female characters, and in fact, the parallels between Alfred Agostinelli and Albertine are unmistakable. On the other hand, Albert Nahmias felt that he and his sisters served as models for Marcel's mistress (Hayman 319). And that is just the point. Proust, as he said repeatedly, used many models for his fictional population, and consequently biographical information, like *La Recherche* itself, holds many possibilities. More convincing, to my mind, is the way in which masculinity seems a mere charade while femininity appears so profoundly rooted in the novel's characters that it ultimately emerges triumphant even after years of being systematically squelched. Albertine and Odette cavalierly don male clothing—it's just another role in the Proustian female's varied repertoire—but Charlus, ladylike man par excellence, struggles unsuccessfully to remain virile as long as he can.

Most critics have ignored this infrastructure of feminine power and have apparently coopted femininity and placed it in a masculine arena. Nonetheless, the patterns which emerge from female experience structure the masterpiece in a most intriguing manner, an organization all the more remarkable given the multiple variations for innumerable passages and the impossibility of a definitive text. They shed new light on Proustian homosexuality and on the narrator's supposed heterosexuality. Indeed, they reveal a sexual economy where femaleness prevails to such a degree that masculinity and heterosexuality are virtually unattainable identities and mothers, or more precisely, Mother is to blame. While many people may inspire each character, all the mothers of *La Recherche*—from the narrator's grandmother to Charlus—have their source in one person—Mme Jeanne Proust. A direct repudiation of the author's mother, the novel insidiously lays bare the flipside of maternal adoration with appropriate Proustian duplicity. In short, to overlook the importance of the novel's female network is to deny a major motor force of *A la recherche du temps perdu*.

Chapter One

Proustian Dichotomy: Good Mothers and Bad (or Where's Papa?)

Although the women of *A la recherche du temps perdu* are incontestably numerous, comprising well over half of the more than five hundred characters, Proust's intention to describe the female psyche is certainly disputable. Yet the novelist not only defines femininity but also gives his definition a binary structure similar to that of the novel itself. Most significant, this dichotomy occurs within a maternal context labeling the prominent women of *La Recherche* (and some men) either good mothers or bad.

Indeed, the narrator's grandmother, as any reader of the novel would confirm, emerges as the most admirable of all Proust's females, and of all the characters in general. Intelligent and cultivated, Mme Amédée has a highly developed ethical as well as aesthetic sensibility, which she communicates to Marcel. And by associating her with Nature, which Proust seemingly admired above human individuals, the writer portrays the grandmother as artless and spontaneous, a woman content to be who she is while never condemning or excluding anything which does not conform to her own experience. Thus, she alone is not a snob. Her loving benevolence is almost universal, and even her disapproval, of alcohol or of Bloch for example, is presented as totally right-minded. Proust comes very close to canonizing this woman who, in her white percale dressing gown that Marcel calls her "habit de religieuse," is a guardian angel ministering to her grandson's anxiety.

And the novelist's ideal woman herself has an ideal, Mme de Sévigné, whose *Lettres* Mme Amédée has read so often that she spontaneously quotes passages—which Proust almost systematically alters. Understandably the grandmother appreciates Mme de Sévigné's love of Nature and regard for others, but most important is this woman's devotion to her daughter. The novelist describes the relationship between Mme de Grignan and her literary mother, though less than perfect in reality, as ideal, exemplifying for the narrator's grandmother *le naturel*. Thus, because Proust sets up Mme Amédée as the one woman by whom all others are judged, her model becomes the ultimate means of evaluating all the other fictional females.

It would seem then that the author of *La Recherche* promotes motherhood as the natural role for women and depicts those who accept and respect it in a flattering light. Women appear to move up and down in the novelist's caste system depending on how well they assume this role. There is, after all, a difference between Odette de Crécy, "cocotte," and Mme de Forcheville, proud mother of socially prominent Gilberte de Saint-Loup, who "sentit qu'elle avait été une bonne et prévoyante mère et que sa tâche maternelle était achevée" and who, defenseless against others' mockery, is for the first time "ce qu'elle n'avait jamais été—infiniment sympathique . . ." (IV, 530). Saint-Loup's mother has this same split personality. Mme de Marsantes is a "mère sainte" when, in the home of Mme de Villeparisis, she regrets reproaching her son Robert for not spending the evening with her ("Voyez-vous, Monsieur, les mères sont très égoïstes" [II, 577]). But she drops dramatically in the Proustian hierarchy when she exchanges her maternal role "pour redevenir grande dame . . ." (II, 579). Mme Cottard, on the other hand, fares quite well for she is one of the few mothers in the novel who approaches this responsibility with such diligence that Dr. Cottard feels obliged to comment, "quand son fils est malade, elle présente des phénomènes d'insomnie" (III, 439). Furthermore, the doctor's wife is the only woman outside the narrator's immediate family who visits his dying grandmother. Her longtime friend, Mme de Villeparisis, never so much as inquires about her health and Mme Amédée's sisters, Flora and Céline, never leave Combray. In fact, Mme Cottard's innate kindness and constant effort to avoid causing pain favor a close resemblance to the narrator's grandmother and mother.

This last equation begs the question of whether the narrator's mother is indeed the equal of her own mother in the Proustian value system. Talk of such symmetry, in my opinion, is not entirely justifiable, although critics tend to speak of the portraits as parallel. To borrow René Girard's term, the grandmother has an external mediator in Mme de Sévigné. There is a distance between the two women which both eliminates rivalry and permits the grandmother to proclaim aloud the true nature of her desire (9): a loving mother-child relationship. Moreover, because the grandmother and her absent mediator are the basis for Proust's hierarchy, they do not have to compete within it, which is not true for the narrator's mother. Her mediator is external but it is the grandmother, not Mme de Sévigné. And though the rivalry normally caused by the nearness of subject and mediator does not exist between the two women, their proximity does make spontaneity in the mother virtually impossible. Relentlessly comparing herself to the grandmother, the narrator's mother vies for position in Proust's hierarchy.

The mother's portrait is thus anticlimactic. The narrator cites her sense of decency, his explanation for her failure to visit Mlle Vinteuil after her father's death, as the only quality which limits her goodness. Yet placed alongside her own mother, their comparable qualities are, in the younger woman, developed to a lesser degree or studied. She simply does not have *le naturel* of the other woman. After the grandmother's death, she does nothing without first deciding what the dead woman would have done in similar circumstances. These otherworldly consultations determine not only which translation of the *Arabian Nights* to buy Marcel but, also, whether to approve his living alone with Albertine in the family's Parisian apartment. In fact, the narrator's mother seems little more than the faithful follower of a cult who, by paying lip-service and by displaying its symbols, hopes to resemble its leader. Conversations about the grandmother become sacred hymns of praise, her belongings become holy relics, and Marcel's mother, who wears her mother's clothing, even looks like the grandmother with the passing years.

She also assumes her mother's admiration for Mme de Sévigné whose volumes are now always with her "exemplaires que ma mère n'eût pas changés contre le manuscrit même des *Lettres*" (III, 167). Ostensibly a sign that the mother has changed the object of her mediation from the grandmother to the maternal role, they serve instead to underscore the mother's continued confusion of the two, and only when the mother thinks solely of the maternal role is she genuine. Significantly, this quality bodies forth during a confrontation between motherhood and snobbishness, a struggle which the latter usually wins because of what the narrator admits to be his mother's preoccupation with social castes. However, for a brief moment in Combray, she thinks only of the parent-child relationship and tries to relax the uncomfortable relations between her family and Swann's after his marriage to Odette: "Voyons, Monsieur Swann . . . parlez-moi un peu de votre fille. . . ." Interrupted, the narrator's mother suggests sympathy for Mme Swann when she adds: "Nous reparlerons d'elle quand nous serons tous les deux, dit-elle à mi-voix à Swann. Il n'y a qu'une maman qui soit digne de vous comprendre. Je suis sûre que la sienne serait de mon avis" (I, 23-24). Here, however briefly, the mother equals the grandmother in goodness.

Yet, motherhood in its traditional form lacks appeal for most Proustian women and the majority would agree with Mme de Villeparisis who, in contrast to the narrator's grandmother, finds Mme de Sévigné's continual concern for her daughter *unnatural* (II, 57). Consequently there is a paucity of conventional mothers in *La Recherche* due in part, I think it fair to say, to Proust's aversion to purely sympathetic portraits. He develops Odette, for example, *in diminuendo* so that as her role of good mother grows, her importance as one of the novel's major characters decreases. Even the narrator's grandmother, who dies before the text has reached its midpoint, and mother diminish in importance and virtually disappear well in advance of the novel's conclusion. Instead, the few women who are represented by the mutual mother-child love of Mme de Sévigné and her daughter are outnumbered and eventually overwhelmed by a second group of females who abuse—or perhaps refuse—the maternal role.

Similar to the first group of women who find their measure in the narrator's grandmother, bad mothers also have a model: the actress Berma whose most notable role, interestingly enough, spotlights misguided motherhood. Only once in *La Recherche* does the actress play anything other than Phaedra, permitting Proust, as he does with *François le Champi,* to underscore his precise intentions through a direct literary allusion. Daughter of Pasiphaë, who had coupled with the white bull to produce the minotaur, Phaedra proves equally aberrant as a mother: she neglects her own children to place her stepson Hippolytus, whom she loves, on the throne. No better as a mother off-stage than on, the actress is self-centered, mocking and unconsciously cruel—"Seulement tout cela, la Berma l'avait immolé à sa fille . . ." (IV, 575). Berma and her dramatic mediator form a perfect negative counterweight to the grandmother and Mme de Sévigné.

While the novelist does not explicitly refer to women who follow in the actress's footsteps as "mères méchantes" (II, 289), Proust's use of the epithet makes it an appropriate title. These are quite simply women who hope to use their progeny for pawn and profit, and they seem to justify Christiane Olivier's observation that "All women play at coming out on top with their children . . . [who] find themselves caught up straightaway in a competitiveness among women" (71). Andrée's mother wants her to marry well and to provide her, as mother-in-law, with all she wants. Mme Bontemps, Albertine's surrogate mother, finds the orphan a useful intermediary in her social advancement. Her young niece's bad manners amuse the aunt and when Albertine replies to a government official's wife claiming ignorance about cooking—"Mais madame . . . vous devriez pourtant savoir ce que c'est, puisque votre père était marmiton" (I, 587-88)—she treats the woman with the insolence Mme Bontemps would have herself liked to use and, furthermore, provides the aunt with an entertaining anecdote for a new audience. Mme Bontemps is openly complicitous when, in Balbec, her niece suggests she dine alone because Albertine is spending a late evening with the narrator: "Mais votre tante sera fâchée?—Pensez-vous! Elle comprendra très bien" (III, 226).

Mme Bontemps understands indeed. When Albertine moves to the narrator's Parisian apartment, she willingly accepts the arrangement while the narrator's mother, although she acquiesces, finds this inappropriate. True to Proustian dichotomy, Marcel's mother and Albertine's aunt have contradictory concepts of their responsibilities: the first woman selflessly indulges her son wishing only his happiness while the second indulges her niece hoping for her own happiness: "Mme Bontemps . . . fermait les yeux sur tout si cela pouvait la débarrasser d'elle en lui faisant faire un riche mariage où un peu de l'argent irait à la tante . . ." (III, 557). The aunt and niece have a business arrangement and, according to Andrée, that is why Albertine eventually leaves the narrator. Mme Bontemps, not believing that Marcel will marry her niece, insists she return to Touraine and not ruin her chances for a profitable marriage with someone else. When the narrator recruits Saint-Loup to offer thirty thousand francs to Mme Bontemps for Albertine's return, Robert reports: "elle n'a pas fait ouf quand j'ai parlé de l'argent" (IV, 55).

This abnormal use of motherhood is legion in the aristocracy. (Sometimes an idiosyncratic motive is added. Mme G, snubbed for years by Mme de Villebon, only wants a Villebon for her daughter.) In fact, the fundamental reason for Odette's eventual success in the Faubourg Saint-Germain, among all her extraordinary efforts, is her daughter. She calls Gilberte "mon trésor" with good reason, for Odette's use of her daughter to force a marriage with Swann is just the beginning (I, 22). Because the child is responsible for the first marriage, she is indirectly responsible for the second. When Swann's death leaves Odette a wealthy woman, the penniless de Forcheville willingly marries her but spends her money far too liberally. Gilberte rescues her mother once again when she becomes the Marquise de Saint-Loup and Robert provides his mother-in-law with the luxuries a spendthrift husband and a pinch-penny daughter deny her: "Elle souhaitait chaque jour un nouveau collier, une nouvelle robe brochée de brillants, une plus luxueuse automobile . . . tout à coup le protecteur elle l'avait flairé, puis trouvé en Robert" (IV, 262).

However, as the Berma paradigm suggests, a malevolent maternal model promotes malevolence in the child. Following Swann's death Gilberte assumes her mother's social ambitions, a goal which compels her to mistreat Odette whom she now sees as a social embarrassment. In his psychoanalytical study of Proust, Milton Miller points out that the girls of *La Recherche* are betrayers who repeat their mother's pattern and mistreat their mothers (290-91). They are a source of humiliation and Odette, like Berma, finds herself sacrificed and degraded with her health endangered by her daughter's desire for social prominence. There is, nonetheless, one key difference here. Berma's daughter bows to her mother's rival Rachel whereas Gilberte vanquishes Odette's. Because she will soon possess the title of Duchesse de Guermantes, she will eclipse Oriane and vindicate her mother's forever being snubbed by this woman.

Oriane de Guermantes herself, condemned ultimately for her spiritual emptiness, does not escape condemnation in Proust's binary definition of femininity either. While the novelist denounces those mothers who abuse their role, he seems to find most reprehensible those women who refuse motherhood altogether. The duchess is not only childless, she appears incapable of the very act necessary for fecundation: the duke left her bed the morning after their wedding never to return (I, 332) and has chosen instead a long series of mistresses. The duke's virility, which clearly marks certain mistresses' children, contrasts impressively with his wife's infertility and makes comprehensible their "mauvais ménage." Yet a closer look reveals that even Oriane momentarily toys with motherhood for she displays the same indulgence for the young Robert de Saint-Loup that do the loving mothers of *La Recherche* for their children. When he dies in combat during World War I Oriane reveals a very rare grief and implies much later, in a conversation with the narrator, that Saint-Loup's death was like the loss of a son (IV, 508). Proust seems to say that emotion emerges only when the duchess plays the maternal role and her moral emptiness corresponds to her refusal of motherhood.

Moreover, the Berma-like woman, whom, because she represents virtually all the women of *La Recherche,* I will refer to simply as the Proustian woman, punctuates her "mauvaise mère" identity by ignoring all family ties and creating, instead, a caste system where these bonds serve only to favor other, more prestigious roles. The Duchesse de Guermantes's title would mean very little to her if she were not also known as the most brilliant hostess in the Faubourg Saint-Germain. On the other hand, women without status, such as Odette, must hide their origins and create an entirely new identity. Berma is, thus, their mediator for a second, more important reason: she is the antithesis of *le naturel*. She is first and foremost an actress. And as Ross Chambers points out, the actress potentially captures all women within her and is consequently situated at the center of what might be called a feminine poetic (74).

Proust agrees wholeheartedly. Proustian characters, male and female, comprise various personae; but no one understands the well-known aphorism "notre personnalité sociale est une création de la pensée des autres" (I, 19) better than the Proustian woman, who actively profits from this psychological phenomenon. That is why, although the novelist passes in review actors of his day—Got, Thiron, Delaunay, Coquelin, etc. as he does actresses—Bernhardt, Bartet, Madeleine Brohan, Jeanne Samary, etc., there are no fictional actors in the novel, only actresses. When the narrator asks Swann what actor Bergotte prefers, he replies: "L'acteur, je ne sais pas. Mais je sais qu'il n'égale aucun artiste homme à la Berma qu'il met au-dessus de tout" (I, 96).

Proust uses the narrator's first view of a Berma performance to punctuate the numerous women that each female comprises. His preconceived idea of the star prompts Marcel to mistake two other women for her. When the actress does appear, she does not correspond to the narrator's image because her interpretation of *Phèdre* is far removed from his reading of the text. The boy uses his grandmother's opera glasses to inspect the star more closely, contrasting the most natural female with the most artificial, and wonders if this image is the true one. By now the narrator has added to his initial idea of the actress four other images and is unable to pinpoint the real Berma.

The novelist goes on to demonstrate how the choice of one of these women as the renowned actress, as with any woman's identity, depends on others' perception. The narrator accepts the actress playing Phaedra as Berma because the audience does: "Enfin éclata mon premier sentiment d'admiration: il fut provoqué par les applaudissements frénétiques des spectateurs" (I, 441-42). And the boy's admiration is further confirmed by M. de Norpois who, dining in the narrator's home for the first time that evening, enumerates the reasons for the actress's success. The boy reflects: "C'est vrai . . . quelle belle voix, quelle absence de cris, quels costumes simples, quelle intelligence d'avoir été choisir *Phèdre*" (I, 449). A final endorsement of Berma's talent appears in *Le Figaro* and the narrator exclaims "Quelle grande artiste!" (I, 472).

The tenuousness of these artificial feminine identities is further exaggerated by their accessibility to all women who wish to duplicate them. Acquisition simply results from mediation: these women choose a model and through systematic imitation hope to take on her persona (Girard 37). Berma did not spontaneously interpret the role of Phaedra, but found models for her performance. Therefore Bergotte points out to the narrator the resemblance between the actress and certain sculptural masterpieces: ". . . elle est bien jolie la petite Phèdre du VIe siècle, la verticalité du bras, la boucle du cheveu qui 'fait marbre' . . . c'est très fort d'avoir trouvé tout ça" (I, 550). Swann, on the other hand, is most impressed with the intonations used as Phèdre said to Œnone "Tu le savais!" Reflecting upon Swann's comment, the narrator unconsciously focuses on the essence of mediation:

> Il restait à la Berma qu'elle l'avait trouvée, mais peut-on employer ce mot de 'trouver', quand il s'agit de quelque chose qui ne serait pas différent si on l'avait reçu, quelque chose qui ne tient pas essentiellement à votre être, puisqu'un autre peut ensuite le reproduire? (I, 557)

However, when the narrator sees Berma a second time, he reacts differently. Seated next to a failed actress who has pledged hatred for the star, Marcel not only witnesses the jealousy of a woman unable to usurp her model but the talent of a successful mediator. He had incorrectly assigned Berma's gift to Racine's genius, for he also sees the actress in an unproven role which would ultimately figure among her greatest: "Je compris alors que l'œuvre de l'écrivain n'était pour la tragédienne qu'une matière, à peu près indifférente en soi-même, pour la création de son chef-d'oeuvre d'interprétation . . ." (II, 351). The narrator had just as incorrectly tried to separate Berma from her role when the key to her success was her ability to become one with it: "Mais ce talent que je cherchais à apercevoir en dehors du rôle, il ne faisait qu'un avec lui . . . ce jeu est devenu si transparent, si rempli de ce qu'il interprète que lui-même on ne le voit plus . . ." (II, 347). For the women of *La Recherche* the capacity to integrate a new, artificial identity decides prominence.

Thus, these women who refuse or abuse motherhood are *all* performers even though, in addition to Berma, only Rachel and Odette are at any time veritable actresses. Rachel remains in this role throughout the novel but is seen primarily as Saint-Loup's mistress and, appropriately enough, demonstrates that her theatrical skills are equally artful off-stage, particularly in the scenes of torture to which she subjects her lover (II, 478). Odette also extends her performance beyond the footlights, initially and most particularly for Swann whom she had met at the theatre while playing the role of Miss Sacripant. Her home's premeditated details suggest the stage's artifice where catleya orchids and chrysanthemums decorate the apartment because they have the great merit of looking artificial (I, 218). Worse, one evening during lovemaking Swann hears a noise and suspects his mistress of soliciting a spectator (I, 366).

Yet it is Odette's wardrobe which provides her most theatrical touch. Indeed, Proust replaces his usually spare physical portrait by a complete catalogue of the actress's apparel, and with the possible exception of Mme de Guermantes, to no other woman does he devote so many descriptive passages. Here Odette is an original. Even as the century draws to a close, the now Mme Swann still evokes the Second Empire, and although she keeps in fashion, she always adds some vestige of another era: "Madame Swann, n'est-ce pas, c'est toute une époque" (I, 608). To display her costumish clothing Odette strolls in the Bois, a world of elegance which focused its ceremonies exclusively upon women (Brée 1955, 84).

The narrator adds Oriane de Guermantes to this group of actresses when he comments on Charlus's distortion of Mme de la Molé's name: "En l'appelant la Molé . . . M. de Charlus lui faisait justice. Car toutes ces femmes étaient des actrices du monde . . ." (III, 780). But whereas Odette uses costume to please her public, Mme de Guermantes—who sees herself as the sole possessor of "l'esprit des Guermantes"—uses good dialogue. The duchess's every affectation of simplicity, from understated dress to feigned ignorance of her social prestige is meant to bring undivided attention to her intelligence. The Faubourg Saint-Germain hostess does this very successfully for to be up-to-date in the *haut monde* one has to know "la dernière d'Oriane." This could be an ingenious play on words (II, 507), an ironic riposte (II, 778), or an impersonation, called "faire des changes" by the Guermantes.

Oriane's most noteworthy performances are given when she contradicts expected Faubourg Saint-Germain behavior. For instance, the duchess makes a point of not attending events considered de rigueur by the rest of society, because as she says to Bloch, "les choses mondaines ne sont pas mon fort" (II, 541). Bloch, taken aback, answers that he thought the reverse to be true. In fact it is, but Mme de Guermantes sees these denials as the true sign of her intelligence, and in a sense, she is right. Seemingly better than anyone she manipulates what Genette terms "le langage indirect." Truth is in the lie; however, the interlocutor is protected by a "truth" which is actually its opposite (Genette 249). Consequently, the real contradiction, typically Proustian, is between Oriane's charming banter and her actions. The result is that, like all her sisters in insincerity, the duchess has no substance:

> Mme de Guermantes a le cœur souvent dur, la pensée souvent faible, mais toujours elle a des signes charmants. Elle n'agit pas pour ses amis, elle ne pense pas avec eux, elle leur fait des signes. Le signe mondain ne renvoie pas à quelque chose, il en 'tient lieu', il prétend valoir pour son sens. Il anticipe l'action comme la pensée, annule la pensée comme l'action, et se déclare suffisant. D'où son aspect stéréotypé, et sa vacuité. (Deleuze 13)

Moreover, to underscore Oriane's true nature, Proust uses a technique which Germaine Brée has observed: he aligns a major character with a secondary one (1955, 234), and thus, infecund flower of the Faubourg Saint-Germain, the Duchesse de Guermantes is eclipsed by the successful actress Rachel at the novel's end.

This misalliance points up an important phenomenon among Proustian women: their metamorphoses through time. After all, when first seen, the roles of these two women are reversed. Oriane is at the height of her power and Rachel is struggling for recognition: ". . . c'est de Mme de Guermantes, qu'elle avait reçu jadis sa plus terrible avanie," for Oriane and her guests had greeted Rachel's recitation with hysterical laughter. "Rachel l'avait peu à peu non pas oubliée mais pardonnée . . ." (IV, 572), and her warmly received performance in the home of the Faubourg Saint-Germain's new queen, the Princesse de Guermantes (Mme Verdurin), vindicates this insult. In addition, Rachel exonerates the years of suffocation from her unavowed mediator's proximity by replacing Berma in the public's esteem.

Rachel's accomplishment is all the more remarkable because she is a former prostitute, something which she never reveals to Saint-Loup even though the narrator recognizes her immediately as "Rachel-quand-du-seigneur" seen years earlier in a *maison de passe*. But the past has no value for the novel's women because they are all busily creating a new identity for the present.[1] Odette is unquestionably the best example of this work in progress. In fact, among all the Proustian women whose emptiness favors numerous identities, Odette undergoes the greatest number of metamorphoses. Given by her mother to a rich Englishman in Nice (a probable explanation for her quasi-familiarity with English), she begins her life as a kept woman early and thus appropriately first appears as the "dame en rose" whom the narrator meets in his Uncle Adolphe's home. Later, she is the

---

[1] This Proustian phenomenon is undoubtedly one of the reasons why Truman Capote saw himself as the American Proust. Capote was drawn to a group of women he called his elegant swans all of whom had beauty, wealth and style. But as Gerald Clarke points out in his biography of the American writer, in truth, these were not the qualities that attracted the author. Instead, he was hypnotized by the story each woman had to tell, and Clarke's comments in this regard could just as easily be about Proust and his fictional women: "Few of them had been born to wealth or position; they had not always glided on serene and silvery waters; they had struggled, schemed and fought to be where they were. They had created themselves, as he himself had done. Each was an artist, he said, 'whose sole creation was her perishable self' " (Clarke, 274).

whom the narrator meets in his Uncle Adolphe's home. Later, she is the "dame en blanc" seen at Tansonville with Charlus. But she is also Miss Sacripant, actress, and Odette de Crécy, "fidèle" of the Verdurin salon. However, as Mme Swann, she is the center of her own salon, and remarried after Swann's death, she is Mme de Forcheville, official member of high society. Odette also has the dubious distinction of being the mistress of many men. The list not only includes the Englishman in Nice but also M. de Crécy, Swann and M. de Forcheville as well as M. de Bréauté, Elstir, D'Osmond and the Duc de Guermantes. Both Charlus and Bloch claim to have enjoyed her favors, and in addition, there are the rumored relationships with Mme Verdurin and other women.

Perhaps la Patronne did not participate in Odette's private life, but Mme Verdurin is unquestionably the model for Odette's public persona. Odette wants a salon comparable to the "petit noyau," and marriage to Swann permits her this. In fact, rivalry with la Patronne probably inspires this union. Odette imitates her mediator and assumes this will establish her "Choufleury": "... elle élevait la voix, lançait les mots, comme elle avait si souvent, dans le petit clan, entendu faire à la 'patronne', dans les moments où celle-ci 'dirigeait la conversation' " (I, 501). Like la Patronne, Odette wants her salon to be known as an intellectual gathering, and her partnership with Bergotte achieves this goal. Soon Mme Swann passes for a superior woman and some even suggest a literary collaboration between woman and writer. Fittingly, Odette returns to the theatre, scene of as many off-stage performances as those on-stage, to ensure her new status: "... ce fut un vrai coup de théâtre quand on vit dans la loge de face, qui était celle de l'auteur, venir s'asseoir à coté de Mme Swann ... la reine du temps, la comtesse Molé" (III, 143).

However, Mme Verdurin, though she does not shed personae with Odette's frequency, makes the most dramatic identity change among Proust's women. She is seen first as the Patronne of the "petit noyau" who secretly covets the Duchesse de Guermantes's power and position in the Faubourg Saint-Germain. Indeed, by the end of the novel, after a brief moment as the Duchesse de Duras, Mme Verdurin, now the Princesse de Guermantes, replaces the duchess as reigning queen of high society. Singlemindedness is one of the reasons for Mme Verdurin's success. Other women target mediators superior in position yet not too far removed from them, and as they overtake and displace one mediator, they move on to a new model, creating this multitude of identities. However, in contrast to other women like her, Mme Verdurin never has her eye on anyone but Oriane.

Yet all of these women, Proust notes, remain fundamentally the same. Each identity change does not mean a basic character change but only a change of circumstances. No one better demonstrates this than the multi-metamorphosed Odette. The Duc de Guermantes's mistress, she remains a "cocotte Second Empire" who with "l'air d'une rose stérilisée" (IV, 528) is still the "dame en rose." The contrast between an inescapably fundamental character and the desire to be other, commonly called *bovarysme* after Gaultier's study, is the root of these women's artificiality. They are, then, the perfect counterpoint to the narrator's grandmother and mother who never wish to change identities.

Indeed, these actresses's every personality trait is explained, not by a desire for parental success, but by their self-interested attempt at social success. For example, Mme Bontemps claims a candor which prohibits this goal: "Moi, quand je vois la femme du ministre de la Guerre faire des grimaces, immédiatement je me mets à l'imiter. C'est terrible d'avoir un tempérament comme ça" (I, 588). But like Mme de Guermantes, she means the opposite of what she says. Albertine's aunt also imitates the duchess's refrain "le monde est assommant" and reveals through this tic and her "langage indirect" that she is moving towards the Faubourg Saint-Germain, for certain modes of expression characterize this milieu as much as titles of nobility do (Genette 260).

Furthermore, self-interest makes these women insensitive and they destroy anyone who impedes their movement to the top. Rachel has her friends persecute another aspiring actress, and when she finally eclipses Berma, Rachel is no less cruel. Finding her rival's child at her feet, she uses the situation to ruin both Berma's prominence and health: ". . . j'ai voulu être plus aimable pour ses enfants qu'elle n'a jamais été pour moi, et pour un peu on m'accuserait de l'avoir assassinée" (IV, 592). On the other hand, socially sure Oriane de Guermantes punishes those who diminish her star quality. She is intent upon penalizing those who have diverted attention from her, whether the Comtesse Molé who imitates her simplicity or Basin's various mistresses. And she punishes Swann for a marriage that necessarily weakens their friendship.

The most important key to these women's character, at once debilitating spiritually and liberating socially, is their inability to love. Far removed from mother-child mutual love, these females function only in business partnerships which move them towards a new persona. This is, of course, not only true for the mother-child relationship, but for relationships between men and women as well. Saint-Loup not only provides Rachel with luxuries she otherwise would not have had but also arranges her first Faubourg Saint-Germain performance. Swann provides Odette with the wealth necessary for a salon whereas the Duc de Guermantes, his wife's public relations man, ensures the prominence of Oriane's. Indeed, the Proustian man's motto "aimer sans être aimé" (Deleuze 16) should be inverted for this group of women: *être aimée sans aimer*. For this reason, if for no other, these females are the antithesis of the author's feminine ideal.

Interestingly, Combray, origin of all the novel's great themes, announces in nascent form this characterization of women. As a contradiction to the loving mother-daughter duo of the narrator's grandmother and mother, Proust gives his readers Marcel's great aunt (the only somewhat vulgar member of his family) and Tante Léonie. In contrast to the first relationship the second seems loveless, and in fact, the great aunt displays little if any sympathy for her daughter's illness. But then Tante Léonie uses theatrics, the celebrated "spectacle dans un lit" to impose her preeminence whereas the narrator's grandmother comes naturally to her role as moral barometer of the novel.

Finally, so powerful is Proust's emphasis on the maternal that it overwhelms the paternal and marks children indelibly, much in the way Mme de Surgis-le-Duc leaves her physical imprint on her two sons Victurnien and Arnulphe. First of all, fathers are few in number: some are soon to die, like Swann; other fathers, such as Saint-Loup's, are dead before the novel begins; and still others, such as the young Marquis himself, simply never appear with their children. Even those father-child relationships which, however short-lived, do appear in the novel—Swann and Gilberte, Vinteuil and his daughter and, of course, the narrator and his father—illustrate unequivocally that when it comes to parenting, daddy is ultimately diminished.

In the case of Mlle Vinteuil and her father, the widowed composer has in fact assumed a maternal role—"Ma mère se rappelait la triste fin de vie de M. Vinteuil, tout absorbée d'abord par les soins de mère et de bonne d'enfant qu'il donnait à sa fille . . ." (I, 157)—obliged as he was to replace the missing mother. Yet the very familiar Montjouvain scene suggests that Mlle Vinteuil continues to seek the absent mother when, with her lesbian companion, she offers her forehead for a kiss "comme elle aurait pu faire si elle avait été sa fille." What is most important about this scene, however, is the way in which the couple blasphemes the father's photograph, and in so doing, "elles allaient ainsi toutes deux au bout de la cruauté en ravissant à M. Vinteuil, jusque dans le tombeau, sa paternité" (I, 161). These females are quite simply rejecting patriarchal law.

Gilberte Swann literally refuses to bear her father's name and like Mlle Vinteuil abuses her father's memory. As a matter of fact, the narrator notes the sincerity of Odette's grief after Swann's death and makes no mention of her daughter's. Welcomed into the Faubourg Saint-Germain thanks to a fortune inherited from Swann's uncle, Gilberte no longer speaks of Swann at all, except in intimate conversations with the narrator. Indeed, when asked outright her father's name, Gilberte claims ignorance of her origin: "On a raconté beaucoup de choses très différentes sur ma naissance, moi je dois tout ignorer" (IV, 165). Gilberte "qui aurait dû rajeunir sinon perpétuer sa mémoire, se trouva hâter et consommer l'œuvre de la mort et de l'oubli" (IV, 172). While the diachronic presentation of Proust's characters makes their unpredictability predictable and thus explains in part Gilberte's eventual disrespect for her father, her mother is also responsible. Both parents have influenced Gilberte's personality, Swann positively and Odette negatively (I, 556), and in the tug-of-war between the paternal and maternal temperament, Swann's finally acquiesces.

The third father-child relationship most dramatically illustrates a repudiation of fatherhood. The narrator's father, one of Proust's shadowy characters remembered primarily for his love of meteorology and association with Norpois, is nameless. Never does his wife use the family name or even assume her husband's first name as does Tante Léonie when called Mme Octave or, more important, as her own mother does as Mme Amédée. Similarly, the narrator eschews the family name and uses, only rarely, Marcel. In fact, the narrator's father is memorable for his very absence. The pivotal Combray "scène du coucher" punctuates his disappearing act while simultaneously underscoring rejection of the Name-of-the-Father. The narrator's mother reads from *François le Champi,* one of the George Sand novels chosen by the grandmother for the boy's birthday, to calm the child into sleep. This novel, in which a foundling is raised by the woman, Madeleine Blanchet, whom he eventually marries, suppresses the paternal entirely. Moreover, the exclusive presence of the mother privileges her as the sole source of naming and, according to Alain Buisine, reflects what transpires in the novel: "Chez Proust la nomination dépend toujours plus ou moins directement de la Mère ou de ses déléguées romanesques" (60). Citing Jean-Pierre Richard's *Proust et le monde sensible* as an example of a critical text that expends some effort to preserve the presence and power of the paternal name, Buisine expresses dismay at a certain refusal to accept "le scandale de l'onomastique proustienne comme désir, visée, commencement d'élaboration d'un système fantasmatiquement matronymique" (62).

The critical refusal to replace the Name-of-the-Father with the Name-of-the-Mother parallels the intransigence of those critics who insist on interpreting the Combray evening when the narrator's mother spent the night in his room as strictly oedipal. First of all, it is acceding to the Name-of-the-Father which delineates the Oedipus Complex and this is clearly something the narrator never does. Furthermore, it seems to me questionable to claim an oedipal relationship between mother and son when the father has made little attempt to end their primary union. Instead of struggling against a son still intimately tied to the Mother, he, by willingly allowing his wife to spend the night with the young Marcel, promotes their intimacy. Thus, this celebrated scene, rather than appearing solely oedipal seems just as justifiably preoedipal, one that highlights the fact that the narrator has never moved beyond the initial mother-child dyad.

In short, fathers are of little consequence. They are overwhelmed by this maternal economy that is the measure of all Proust's female characters and, as men, find themselves either in a secondary role, ultimately dominated by the maternal, or metamorphosed into the maternal. There is even evidence of the same good mother/bad mother bifurcation among men. The self-sacrificing "bonne d'enfant" that is the biological father Vinteuil clearly contrasts with the self-interested, self-appointed parent Charlus who hopes to advance Morel's career and to bring favor on his sexual advances with the young man at the same time. Furthermore, that the maternal role means everything in Proust's novel, signals simultaneously the importance of the preoedipal and, to my mind, provides the appropriate economy in which to evaluate Marcel's future relationships, indeed, the way he views all women.

Chapter Two

The Proustian Mother and Object Relations Theory

The narrator's preoccupation with the maternal figure belies an understanding of a phenomenon that feminists interested in psychoanalysis, and as unhappy with Freud's rejection of the Mother as with his penis-envy theory, have recently brought to the foreground: the mother-child relationship, beyond all else, leaves an inescapable imprint on everyone's psyche. Parenting patterns which make women the primary caretaker of children privilege this experience, particularly in the bourgeois model, and favor a domestic unit that is admittedly male dominant but, nonetheless, father absent (Chodorow 3-5).

Certainly the narrator's family adheres to this paradigm and reflects it in exaggerated form, for at the end of the nineteenth century the maternal role was by no means limited to physical care of the child. On the contrary, mothers were supposed to inculcate good manners in their children and to teach them the intellectual, moral and religious rules necessary for psychological equilibrium and social success (Sagaert 113). M. Chambon advises in his manual, *Le Livre des Mères,* that a mother must begin this education by setting the example herself (181), and she is, notes Louis Bondivienne in a book published three years after Proust's birth, "la première et la plus indispensable institutrice de ses enfants . . ." (180). It is in this Mother-knows-best world that Proust lived and that appears in his quasi-autobiographical novel.

Indeed, Proust's very inability to identify totally with or to distinguish himself completely from the narrator makes it virtually impossible not to confuse the two. Inevitably, biographical information bodies forth to support or contradict a whole host of notions about the author's masterpiece. Nonetheless, nowhere is it more appropriate to do so, it seems to me, than in the instance of the narrator's experience of the Mother. I am not about to suggest that *A la recherche du temps perdu* contains a simple transposition of the celebrated Jeanne Weil Proust/Marcel Proust relationship but that, because the author himself believed that one's daily affective life is the point of departure for creation, the person who consumed his affection also permeated Proust's unconscious—the source of his novel. Whether, as Martine Sagaert observes, the maternal "se présente à l'écrivain comme modèle ou comme anti-modèle, il fonctionne comme matériau-vie. Tantôt sacralisé, tantôt profané, n'est-il qu'un prétexte, prétexte-à-parler de Soi, prétexte-à-LITTÉRATURE?" (130).

Object relations theory promises fresh insights into this universe where Mother prevails. Although dependent on Freud and in agreement with his emphasis on sexuality, it is a psychoanalytic perspective which, nonetheless, does not reduce the child to instinct (nor does it privilege direct environmental determinism). Rather it sees a personal subject with ego potential in whom psychic structures arise from the self's experience of objects, all that which is perceived as not itself. And, according to this theory, the child's social relational experience from earliest infancy determines psychological growth and personality formation (Chodorow 47). This last notion prompts three significant shifts in emphasis. In contrast to Freud who sees the oedipal stage (ages 3 to 6) as essential to character formation, object relations stresses the preoedipal period (ages 1 to 3). This interval encompasses the developmental processes of symbiosis, separation/individuation and transitional space. Secondly, while not denying the importance of the oedipal stage, this theory places the preoedipal, which orthodoxy sees as pre-gendered, above the oedipal as the source of gender identification. This change in focus is possible because gender differences are seen to have social causes which begin with the child's relationship to its primary caretaker. Finally, and most important, because women almost always assume this caretaking responsibility the Mother effectively replaces the Father as key to a child's psychic development.

Psychic structures are socially constituted through a series of object choices which depend on the personality and behavior of those who interact with the child. What is internalized becomes unconscious and persists more or less independent of the original relationship. This internalization is not a direct transmission of the child's external world but, instead, involves distortion, defenses and transformations (Chodorow 50). Internalizations build upon one another, inform and conflict with one another. And because unconscious object worlds developed during childhood continue to affect adult external experiences, these inner worlds—and accompanying conflicts—are imposed upon and give meaning to external situations. Adults unconsciously recreate, and are often unable *not* to recreate, aspects of their early relationships, most notably if they are unresolved, ambivalent and repressed (Chodorow 51). In short, all people live their past partly in the present, and more important, this past is anchored in the gendered pre-oedipal experience of the Mother.

Thus, Proust's experience with his own mother plays an ineluctably key role in the organization of a novel that, unequivocally, sets out to capture the past. Jeanne Weil Proust and Marcel formed a uniquely close pair, even by late nineteenth century bourgeois standards. During those first years following Proust's birth on July 10, 1871, his mother was excessively attentive. Biographers Hayman and Painter alike believe these attentions might have been due to her guilt over a difficult pregnancy, the psychological and physical pressures she had undergone throughout the nine months. The Parisian winter had been so cold the Seine froze; food had been so scarce that people ate dogs, cats and rats; there was street fighting after the Prussian army, having signed an armistice with France, had marched down the Champs-Elysées; and worst of all, her husband, Dr. Adrien Proust, had almost been struck by a bullet (Hayman 4). Mme Proust felt that Marcel had been indelibly marked and constitutionally weakened and her culpability virtually prevented her from letting him out of her sight.

In fact, normal symbiosis, the veritable oneness of mother and child which ordinarily lasts only through the infant's first six or seven months, appears extraordinarily extended in the case of Marcel and his mother. By now even those who have only limited knowledge of Proust and his work know of the narrator's devotion to his mother—or perhaps even of the questionnaire where the adolescent Marcel revealed that his greatest unhappiness was separation from Mme Proust. Yet this need was mutual. In his biography, Hayman characterizes the couple's relationship as "symbiotic" and notes that Mme Proust "wanted to share everything in his [Marcel's] life" (Hayman 31). Not even her second child Robert intruded on this exclusiveness: "Fierce and possessive, the mutual adoration of young mother and ailing boy made the placid, healthy baby a pig-in-the-middle. She called Marcel 'mon petit loup' and Robert 'mon autre loup' " (Hayman 6).

That Jeanne Proust should use *autre* to designate her younger child is not without significance. Robert *was the Other,* a child whose primary union with the mother was shorter-lived and whose ultimate similarity to his father (both were doctors) makes clear his use of paternal identification to separate eventually from the female parent. Marcel, by contrast, was the child who so distinctly resembled his mother that mutual absorption of Subject and Other made any real existence of otherness out of the question. Nothing seemed more desirable to the boy Marcel than, for example, to talk and write like Mme Proust, that is to say with a maximum of quotations and classical allusions, even though his classmates (and teachers) found his preciosity laughable (Hayman 25). This mutual identification in which the author seeks his self in the mother is evident in the narrator's experience as well: Marcel remarks, ". . . ma mère et ma grand-mère, mes modèles en tout . . ." (II, 144). And Leo Bersani, in a study of Proust which implicitly substantiates object relations theory and the role of the Mother, points out that Marcel's nightly need for the maternal presence reveals that "his self is with his mother and he must have her in order to have it" (49), behavior he repeats as an adult. The narrator sees the mother as his *sosie,* not only the physical equivalent that Odette discovers when comparing two photographs on Oncle Adolphe's desk (I, 75), but also the ideological, intellectual, and physical "identical twin" that Mme Jeanne Proust was to her son. Commenting on the author after his mother's death Martine Sagaert notes: "Celui qui s'identifiait à sa mère et qui voulait vivre en symbiose avec elle, blotti dans ses bras, pourrait redire cette prière de 1904: 'Nous ne ferons qu'une personne comme nous ne faisons qu'un cœur . . .' " (126).

This fusion of mother and child is the paradigm for Marcel's relationship between self and world: whether *aubépines* or Albertine, each absorbs the other. Ghislaine Florival, whose *Le désir chez Proust* suggests a metaphysics of desire, continually returns to this pattern of oneness in her discussion of the narrator's connection to his universe. She observes that the child, and then the adult, wishes to love and be loved in return and goes back to the origin of its existence to create this mutuality. Furthermore, loving and knowing are ultimately tied to this same source:

> Si le désir affectif renvoie aux origines maternelles, à la fusion dans la nature originaire, le désir intellectuel vise la totalité, l'union dans l'Etre . . . réciproquement, la recherche de l'Etre se fonde nécessairement dans ce premier désir, le retour aux sources de la vie . . . L'enfant souhaite la fusion maternelle, c'est-à-dire qu'il désire se perdre dans l'unité première, dans la Nature-Mère. (7)

However, the appropriateness of such a seamless mother-child couple is questionable, for the good infant caretaker relationship should develop a sense of basic relatedness *and a sense of separate self* at the same time. During the preodipal period individuation/separation—which may last until the child is two (Flax 176)— should succeed symbiosis, and ego boundaries (an understanding of the personal psychological distinction from the rest of the world) and a bounded body ego (the perception of permanent physical separateness and of the predictable boundedness of the body) emerge (Chodorow 68). The mirror stage marks the beginning of this process and here the Mother's role is incomparable. In contrast to Lacanian theory which characterizes this stage as the moment when the infant proleptically takes on a cohesive identity through the mediation of a mirror and the Other, embodied *perhaps* by the Mother (Gallop 80), Winnicott focuses on the Mother as mirror. The child sees itself when looking into the Mother's gaze and ideally sees an organized, cohesive being. The psychoanalyst thus inserts ego development into object relations, and in addition, makes the Mother virtually omnipotent (Sprengnether 185).

And yet, in the case of each Marcel the *glace* that is the Miroir/Mère, while it resembles Winnicott's, resembles Irigaray's as well. Both children see a cohesive image but the image is so like that of the Mother that it is immobilizing: "Avec ton lait, ma mère, j'ai bu la glace [Obviously, Irigaray is profiting from the double meaning ice/mirror] . . . Tu as coulé en moi, et ce liquide chaud est devenu poison qui me paralyse" (Irigaray 1979, 7). The two Marcels seem unsuccessful in the disidentification process necessary to a boy's psychic development. This is not surprising in an object relations context. Because of the initial symbiotic state in which mother and child represent a dual unity, this theory posits implicitly, if not explicitly, primary femininity for all children. This, of course, enhances a girl's identity whereas, for the boy, it makes the path to masculinity quite problematic. Consequently, according to Robert Stoller, there are many more biologically normal males whose gender is unambiguously female than there are biologically normal females who see themselves as male (358). This reverses Freud's claim of psychological primacy for masculinity (the little girl is a "little man" theory), and in this manner object relations suggests that gender identity is a precondition of the Oedipus Complex.

Furthermore, because, as psychoanalytic clinical findings have shown, there is nothing natural or preordained in the development of human sexuality, parents play a major role in the construction and enforcement of sexual orientation and its definition. Heterosexual orientation calls for children to identify with the parent of the same sex. This means that a boy's heterosexuality is necessarily at risk because "his still-to-be-created masculinity is endangered by the primary, profound, primeval oneness with mother, a blissful experience that serves, buried but active in the core of one's identity, as a focus which, throughout life, can attract to regress back to that primitive oneness" (Stoller 358). Clearly this is significant for Proust and the narrator, both of whom choose a member of the opposite sex—the Mother—as the model for their own gender identification.

Of course, the Mother herself is all powerful in the separation/individuation process which ultimately leads to her child's choice of gender and sexual orientation. On the one hand the mother who controls a child's environment for too long prevents the child from developing the relational capacities or sense of being at the core of the central ego (Chodorow 83). Bersani demonstrates how this is true for the narrator. But Marcel exhibits another result of overdetermined mothering: his strategies for dealing with anxiety are inadequate. Certainly there are those critics, most notably Deleuze, who prefer to see Swann as responsible for the narrator's *angoisse:* ". . . nous rencontrons Swann qui, venant dîner à Combray, prive l'enfant de la présence maternelle. Et le chagrin du héros, son angoisse à l'égard de sa mère, c'est déjà l'angoisse et le chagrin que Swann lui-même éprouvait pour Odette . . ." (88). But it seems to me that the Mother is inevitably responsible. Swann's appearance at the family dinner table separates Marcel from his mother but had she helped her child more efficaciously with the separation/individuation process, in particular had she not acquiesced when her husband suggested she spend the night in Marcel's room, Swann would not have been able to provoke the boy's anxiety.

Indeed, the celebrated *scène du coucher* is key for the role it plays in the separation/individuation process. It illustrates how the narrator's mother does not expressly push her son out of his preoedipal attachment into an oedipally marked one. Willpower is what the narrator feels he has lost forever on that momentous evening: no longer will he attempt to pull *apart* from his mother but will remain *a part* of her instead. Thus, even *François le Champi* must be read differently, and in contrast to those who see the George Sand novel as an incest narrative. It seems to me, because the mother systematically suppresses all the love scenes when reading the novel aloud to Marcel ("quand c'était maman qui me lisait à haute voix . . . elle passait toutes les scènes d'amour" [1, 41]), that it is the simple story of an uninterrupted union between mother and child.

Of course, it is possible to suggest that the mother's efforts at separation, though decidedly late, occur when the narrator travels to Balbec without her. In fact, the narrator comments that it is this experience which proves that his mother could live without him and not simply for him. However, Marcel travels to the sea resort with his grandmother and thereby demonstrates how intimately tied to the Mother he remains. Furthermore, it is no accident that the novel the narrator pulls out when perusing books indiscriminately in the Prince de Guermantes's library at the novel's close is *François le Champi* and resuscitates the child he once was: "Aussi ce livre que ma mère m'avait lu haut à Combray presque jusqu'au matin, avait-il gardé pour moi tout le charme de cette nuit-là" (IV, 463). Appropriately, *François le Champi* creates a bookend effect which signals the primary union it symbolizes as the crucial experience which launches the novel. Indeed, the mother's inability to push her son out of the preoedipal attachment will ultimately jeopardize his masculinity and preclude heterosexual sexual orientation.

This mother unwilling to encourage separation/individuation and for whom, the narrator pointedly remarks, "j'étais toujours un enfant" (IV, 509) was certainly Jeanne Weil Proust. Hayman reveals the somewhat breathtaking fact that Proust was still using baby talk with his mother at the age of sixteen (29), and similar to the narrator's mother, she seems to have impaired Proust's early relational capacities or sense of being. Hayman says of Proust: "With his insecure hold on his identity, he felt terrified he'd lose himself unless he could tether his reality to something in the world outside. Looking intently at roses or hawthorn bushes or trees, he's trying to take possession of something neither wholly external nor wholly internal" (97). And the neurasthenia that Proust seemed to have inherited from his Tante Elisabeth (Tante Léonie in the novel) was the very reification of his anxiety, causing him to do everything from wearing a fur coat indoors—and probably with long underwear beneath his tuxedo—to going long stretches of time without eating.

Proust's father, who had an abundance of willpower, might have provided him with the strength necessary to extricate himself from his neurasthenia and overly protective and possessive Mother. However, the author was unable to identify with Dr. Adrien Proust and remained instead under the sway of the female parent. This in part explains his effeminacy and homosexuality. Because a child's oedipal stance depends on the inner object world it *brings to* and uses during the oedipal period (Chodorow 64—emphasis added), Proust moved halfheartedly into phallic competition with his father—who was as flexible as the narrator's that pivotal Combray evening. Dr. Adrien Proust believed, as he explained in his own books on childrearing, that attempts at discipline could be counterproductive. Nonthreatening, he proved just as inconsequential in the child's resolution of the Oedipus Complex as was the fictional father whom the grandmother found too soft on Marcel. Clearly the Law of the Father was not in play for the narrator. He perceives his father to be without the firmly held principles of the grandmother—". . . il n'avait pas à proprement parler d'intransigeance" (I, 36). But the narrator understands that his father's behavior is in large part due to his inability to understand Marcel the way the mother and grandmother do. Indeed, had he better understood his son he would not have allowed his wife to spend the night in Marcel's room; he would not have allowed the boy to see *Phèdre;* and he would not have permitted him to forgo a diplomatic career. Ironically, though, these three lapses in patriarchal power are crucial to the elaboration of Marcel's novel.

Because the Mother's dominion is virtually absolute, preoedipal issues seem, at the very least, to intertwine with the oedipal, but more often they seem to overwhelm them. In this respect the narrator and Proust alike give the impression of following female psychic development, a phenomenon that would support Appignanesi's view of Proust's essential femininity or, for that matter, Doubrovsky's notion that the narrator really wants to be a woman. Certainly as young boys they seemed to relate better to girls—Proust with Marie de Benardaky et al. on the Champs-Elysées and the narrator with Albertine and "la petite bande." Mme Blatin even wanted to suggest to the narrator's mother that he was "too pretty" to be a boy (I, 406). The interpenetration of mother and child which characterizes both is used by Irigaray to capture mothers and daughters. The two Marcels, similar to females, have not resolved their Oedipus Complex, in their case because they have refused all identification with the Father. And like girls, they struggle with a prolonged and painful severance from the Mother. In addition, passivity, masochism, and narcissism, which are more frequently female solutions to anxiety or guilt (Chodorow 152) because the generating mother-child pattern is more typically a mother-daughter experience, are common to the narrator and Proust. For both, the inability to move to action—to write their novel, the incapacity to understand love except through suffering, and their ultimately narcissistic rather than anaclytic choice of love object bear witness to a feminine psychic development.

Moreover, themes associated with preoedipal issues permeate *La Recherche*. Anxiety is omnipresent in Marcel's apprehensive desire for the goodnight kiss, whether the Mother's or Albertine's; intense and exclusive attachment to the Mother is systematically repeated in the narrator's choice of the beloved, in what Deleuze calls his love series; the importance of orality and food is so widespread and well known that it needs no explanation; and maternal control of the child's body is evidenced by the narrator's unwillingness to place himself amidst the book's inverted males (and by Proust's choice to write and publish a novel generously peopled with homosexuals only after his mother's death). Moreover, the primacy of the preoedipal is surely one of the essential reasons that Proust is perceived as a "feminine" writer. In short, this period, as it is for females, seems the primary building block in his psychic structure.

This prolonged preoedipal period, however, does for Proust and the narrator exactly what it does for females. It creates intense ambivalence toward the Mother. Chodorow, in fact, insists on the length and the intensity of this stage—not Freudian penis-envy—as the source of female ambivalence which causes girls to turn away from the Mother in the oedipal stage. Proust and the narrator seem to follow the same path. They eventually seek freedom from dependence and merging and will attempt to escape this preoedipal mother Chasseguet-Smirgel calls phallic (171-82), not because of the Mother's perceived physiology, but because of her power. Thus although both Marcels literally possess the male sex organ, they, like females, will react to the powerlessness of primary identification and maternal omnipotence and will seek the power and freedom it promises in order to become autonomous individuals.

This ambivalence is clear in Proust's life and Hayman recounts a variety of details that reveal how mother and son alike behaved spitefully, unreasonably and moved back and forth between loving closeness and angry resentfulness. In the novel, the narrator does not hide his mother's fits of anger, noting that his mother might not speak to him for days. As a boy, the author declared he hated his mother when, clearly jealous, she intervened in his friendship with Marie de Benardaky and decided with her husband that it would have to end because of Marcel's perpetual overexcitement (Hayman 31). She is this same interventionist for the narrator, although in a similar situation she is shown in a more flattering light. When the bedridden boy is demoralized by no word from Gilberte, he suspects his mother of asking her to write when he finally receives a letter. At twenty-five Proust turned his schedule upside down, slept all day and went out at night, permitting him the luxuries of his mother's care while preventing her too much knowledge of his emotional and social relationships (Hayman 115). Financially dependent on his parents Proust took perverse pleasure in flaunting his extravagances in front of his mother who kept close watch over his expenses and saw this arrangement as an essential part of their symbiosis (Hayman 136). And when, after her husband's death and Robert's marriage, Mme Proust was weak and depressed, Proust seemed maliciously satisfied with her dependence on him (Hayman 202). Nonetheless, she still kept him virtually under her thumb until she died in 1905 when Proust was thirty-four.

Ambivalence towards the Mother in Proust's novel is rarely a literal translation of events such as these but rather takes a decidedly more perverse form. Maliciousness metamorphoses into malevolence. On the surface all is well and the narrator and his mother (and grandmother, for Proust took real life information about the women and conflated their portraits) rarely reflect anything but the very best qualities in the couple that were Proust and his mother. However, the death of Jeanne Weil Proust, the author's looking-glass, permitted her son to see the pair in a way that was not necessarily her vision of the two. His mother's death convinced Proust that one never experiences anything except retrospectively (Hayman 231) and consequently allowed the author to examine their relationship in a new light, through his imagination rather than simply his senses.

Indeed, in contrast to George Painter whose biography stresses the repression Jeanne Proust imposed on her son, Hayman cannot insist strongly enough on the key role she plays in the elaboration of Proust's masterpiece. The first two pages of preliminary jottings for *La Recherche*, which date from 1908, show just how connected the task was to the author's mother. A quotation from Thomas Carlyle's confessions to his mother—'I am not so ill as I tell you'—is followed by notes on a dream in which the novelist's mother is resuscitated (Hayman 274). "The compulsion to re-enact experiences of frustration coalesced with guilt about all the vengeful fantasies he'd aimed against her. Still mourning her death and blaming himself for overloading her with anxiety about his health, he was trying to stabilize his thoughts and dreams about her through a literary recreation of their relationship" (Hayman 296). The feelings that his mother provoked at this point in his life were, appropriately enough, as potent as they had been when, as a child, he was separated from her.

That he was obsessed with Mme Proust after her death is clear in a comment made by the author, a statement just as easily attributable to the narrator's mother about Mme Amédée: "I do not stop thinking about her for a moment, even while sleeping, I see her near me all the time, do not stop interrogating her about everything I do, and believe I hear her answering me" (Hayman 233-34). Having spent his life in a maternal space, Proust did not want to abandon it. But the apartment he had shared with his mother on the rue de Courcelles contained far too many memories. His maternal great uncle Louis Weil's apartment, however, did not, and thus the novelist decided to sublet these rooms at 102, Boulevard Haussmann because, while they were very familiar to Jeanne Proust, they did not overwhelm her son with painful recollections. Proust crammed as much of the family furniture as possible into the space and hung a portrait of his mother by Mme Beauvois in the drawing-room. He slept in the bedroom where Oncle Louis had died, thinking it would bring him closer to his mother, and he kept a variety of family photos there—some of the people Proust did not know but his mother had loved. The author even had wanted to use his mother's bedroom furniture but thought better of it after considering how any residual talcum powder might exacerbate his asthma.

The adherence to a maternal site which orients Proust after his mother's death and which literally represents the place where he begins *A la recherche du temps perdu* corresponds to the space which opens the novel itself. The multiple confusions—"... j'étais moi-même ce dont parlait l'ouvrage ..." (I, 3); "... les meubles, la chambre, le tout dont je n'étais qu'une petite partie ..."; and "... une femme naissait pendant mon sommeil d'une fausse position de ma cuisse" (I, 4) for example—mark the first few pages with an interpenetration reminiscent of mother and child. Indeed, the narrator appears to recapture primary union: "... j'avais seulement dans sa simplicité première, le sentiment de l'existence comme il peut frémir au fond d'un animal ..." (I, 5). And winter ("... chaude caverne creusée au sein de la chambre même ..." [I, 7]) or summer ("... on aime être uni à la nuit tiède ..." [I, 7]) the bedroom in which the narrator finds himself is the same symbiotic environment that permitted Proust to realize his self while his mother was alive and that will allow him, through writing his monumental work, to realize who, in truth, he is. Comparable to Tante Léonie, he establishes his power there.

Son of an overcontrolling mother, Proust may choose to remain merged with the Mother or reject her. Though extraordinarily difficult, there are early signs that, while beginning his rite of passage toward self-understanding merged with the mother in a comfortable maternal space, the author attempts to move away from her. The novel abounds with a strategy that the male child uses in the separation/individuation process—fetishism, which results from boundary confusion and a lack of sense of self firmly distinguished from his mother (Chodorow 107). Marcel's most salient fixation—as many have remarked and most notably Doubrovsky—is on the Mother's cheek. Fittingly it is during a scene of literal separation, when Swann's arrival obliges the boy to return to his room, that he employs this strategy: "Aussi je me promettais, dans la salle à manger, pendant qu'on commencerait à dîner et que je sentirais approcher l'heure, de faire d'avance de ce baiser qui serait si court et furtif, tout ce que j'en pouvais faire seul, de choisir avec mon regard la place de la joue que j'embrasserais ..." (I, 27). Perhaps even more significant, a subtle reference to the Mother appears in the first few pages of *La Recherche* when the narrator describes "les belles joues de l'oreiller" (I, 4).

Moreover, the Proustian dichotomy which permeates the novel and separates women into good mothers and bad is but another strategy Proust uses to move away from the Mother and cope with his ambivalence. He uses object splitting and allows the narrator, on the one hand, to internalize the nurturing and protective maternal figure and, on the other hand, the author compels him to introject an image of the mother as rejecting and denying gratification: the mother who offers the goodnight kiss contrasts neatly with the mother who denies it. By splitting the object so that the mother has both good and bad qualities, Proust launches a struggle between these two females to see who will prevail.

And yet there is no mystery here. Proust uses his preoedipally marked novel of symbiosis and separation as a type of transitional space to do what he could never do when his mother was alive. Proust rejects her by profaning her memory, offering up the textual equivalent of showing (so rumor has it) photographs of his mother at a male brothel and prompting acquaintances to ask him who was the whore (Hayman 428).

Chapter Three

Albertine à la Dinnerstein

Nowhere is the nefarious impact of mothering more prominent than in the narrator's relationship with Albertine. An amalgam of contradictions and the most mysterious of Proust's characters, Albertine reveals, nonetheless, the pattern of Marcel's love, his "répétition amoureuse" (Deleuze 85). Because this repetition is a product of the narrator's mind, an imaginative construct with which he invests each female, she is both different and similar, converging in some way with every other woman loved by the narrator. (The conflation of her portrait with Gilberte's is the most prominent example.) Indeed, Albertine is their hyperbolic representative for within her characterization the attempt to collapse Mother and Lover is most evident.

That the Mother is ineluctably the inspiration for Marcel's love series seems to me undeniable, although, as I have already pointed out, Deleuze himself sees, instead, Swann as the source of the paradigm. This displacement of the Mother is, to my mind, inappropriate, not only because the Mother herself rather than the dilettante initiates anxiety the critic thinks essential but because it privileges disquietude over the tranquility of primary love. The search for symbiosis is what propels the narrator through his love series and Swann's absence would make no perceptible difference in this quest. It is true that the parallels between the narrator and Swann are exhaustively well known and Swann might even see in Odette the maternal similarity that Marcel seeks in the beloved: ". . . cette Odette sur le visage de qui il avait vu passer les mêmes sentiments de pitié pour un malheureux, de révolte contre une injustice, de gratitude pour un bienfait, qu'il avait vu éprouver autrefois par sa propre mère . . ." (I, 263). Nonetheless, only

Marcel's relationship to Albertine brings these similarities to light. And even this relationship has some noteworthy differences—for example, Marcel lives with his companion, as he himself points out, while he still loves her. Most important, though, lesbianism never plays the role for Swann and Odette that it does for Marcel and Albertine. Swann suspects Odette of lesbian activity but he seems appropriately more jealous of men because it is with men that Odette most often surrounds herself. This contrasts dramatically with Albertine who has almost exclusively female friendships, a phenomenon that ultimately has great bearing on Marcel's most important love relationship. But more seductive is the resemblance to the Mother—and the mutual love she represents—among all those females loved by the narrator. Florival argues: "Le désir apparaît donc comme négation de l'angoisse. L'abîme néantisant se transforme alors en puissance d'être, en intention non encore actualisée, mais qui est promesse de plénitude, possession déjà imaginaire d'une totalité retrouvée. La mère est au cœur du désir" (44).

Consequently, the narrator frequents the same mother figures that Proust sought himself, among whom, appropriately enough, Mme Emile Straus served as a model for both Mme de Guermantes and Odette. Oriane, while she attracts Marcel with beauty, wit and prestige also does so through the safety of her age. And in the case of Mme Swann, the narrator imitates the novelist's "passionate but puppyish efforts to win affection from his friends' mothers" (Hayman 55). Indeed, in the Swann family Odette holds as much interest for the young Marcel as does Gilberte (the opening pages of *A l'ombre des jeunes filles en fleurs* are, after all, entitled "Autour de Mme Swann"), and still in love with Mlle Swann, the narrator's affections seem to fluctuate between mother and daughter. Furthermore, watching Mme Swann stroll in the Bois de Boulogne the narrator tries to link himself to the young girl through contact, however tenuous, with the mother. He seems to understand instinctively a phenomenon that feminists such as Irigaray and Chodorow have only recently proposed: mothers and daughters are virtually interchangeable.

This explains why Marcel continues to visit Odette once he and Gilberte are no longer on good terms: ". . . quand j'allais faire à Mme Swann une de ces tristes visites où, lui ayant de par mon chagrin, retrouvé toute sa mystérieuse poésie de mère de cette Gilberte à qui elle dirait le lendemain: 'Ton ami m'a fait une visite'. . ." (I, 585). Now, rather than building an association with Mlle Swann, he is prolonging its end, and in both cases, the narrator turns to Odette. However, another interpretation of "toute sa mystérieuse poésie de mère" is still more appropriate. Because in this his initiation to love Marcel discovers that the beloved does not necessarily return affection, he turns to the woman who symbolizes the only successful love experience he has known. Thus, when the narrator later explains that the hypothetical character around which he constructs Albertine's personality is Mme Swann's, he is not only referring to her mendacity and the multiplicity of women she comprises but also to the mother that the Balbec adolescent will eventually represent.

Moreover, within the "petite bande" it is the maternal role which promotes the greatest confusion between Andrée and Albertine who, appearing last in a parade of young girls, provides a visual metaphor for the love series. Andrée, older and wiser than the other adolescents, is particularly protective of Albertine, calling her Titine or "ma petite" as a mother might a child. Also, saying that it wouldn't be "protocolaire," she expresses an indignation typical of most mothers when the narrator says he'll be visiting Albertine in her hotel room. But while she exhibits qualities associated with Proust's good mothers, Andrée, at the same time, behaves in typical bad mother fashion by prefiguring the questionable character of her friend. Albertine seems quite puerile during Marcel's first summer at the Normandy resort but, by the second, equals Andrée in dissemblance and unpredictability. And they appear to exhibit the same interpenetration that do Mme Swann and her daughter: ". . . Andrée . . . était tout de même une amie d'Albertine, partageant sa vie . . . au point que le premier jour je ne les avais pas distinguées d'abord l'une de l'autre" (II, 296).

Indeed, while Marcel's love for both (". . . l'amour avait été alternatif et par conséquent, en somme, il n'y en avait eu qu'un à la fois" [IV, 87]) favors their interchangeability, the continual Andrée/Albertine transposition is, more significantly, an amplification of the theme in Marcel's earlier relationship with Gilberte and Mme Swann: the young man's love once again hesitates between "mother and daughter," but this time, because of their respective ages, the narrator can pursue Andrée in a way he could not pursue Odette. However, the pattern is the same. Marcel first associates himself with the daughter through the mother (walks in the Bois to see Mme Swann/initial pursuit of Andrée); during the love relationship itself the mother serves as a defense against any possible pain caused by the beloved ("Cet aveu à Albertine d'un sentiment imaginaire pour Andrée . . . je pus enfin, sans crainte qu'Albertine y soupçonnât de l'amour, lui parler avec une douceur que je me refusais depuis si longtemps et qui me parut délicieuse" [III, 224-25]); and finally, Odette and Andrée serve to extend each relationship but, in so doing, allow the narrator to end his painful love association with Gilberte and Albertine.

Ultimately though, these two couples are but preparatory stages in a project for which Albertine is the third and culminating moment. No longer does Marcel attempt to meet his ends by playing one female off another but instead hopes to achieve his goal of mutual love within one person. To do this Marcel must reconcile the conflicting groups of women that comprise the Proustian dichotomy. On one side of the equation there are those women, the good mothers, who are capable of love but inaccessible sexually. In contradistinction are those who refuse or abuse motherhood, Proustian women, who are sexually accessible but incapable of love. The narrator hopes that the Balbec adolescent will, like the Mother, be capable of love. Certainly he has already seen signs of her sexual availability: ". . . Albertine avait une prononciation si charnelle et si douce que, rien qu'en vous parlant, elle semblait vous embrasser" (II, 656).

Indeed, there is no mistaking Albertine's similarity to the Proustian woman. Ringleader of the "petite bande" she is comparable to Mme Verdurin with her "petit noyau," essential to the closed club's very existence: ". . . et peut-être cette attraction qu'Albertine exerçait bien involontairement avait-elle été à l'origine, avait-elle servi à la fondation de la petite bande" (II, 287). Often invited into the homes of people her friends' mothers see as considerable, the young woman, like the Duchesse de Guermantes, has no need to make herself available or to make known her social success. And "actrice de la plage," like all other actresses, Albertine is capable of leading the hostess to believe, as well as any friends who might be there, that it is only for each of them that she has come to a particular social event.

Albertine's ability to assume the contradictory role in Proust's system is not so clear, and the narrator, when he requests that she attend a performance of *Phèdre*,[1] seems to suggest that she assume the role of mother

---

[1] I think it quite curious that when, as a child, the narrator read what plays were in town on the "colonnes Morris" he was not allowed to choose among "une de ces œuvres étranges comme *Le Testament de César Girodet* ou *Œdipe-Roi*" (I, 73) but was permitted

as well as lover. Not coincidentally, Marcel compares Albertine to his mother for the first time when the young woman cancels plans to see him after the play:

> En entendant ces mots d'excuse, prononcés comme si elle n'allait pas venir, je sentis qu'au désir de revoir la figure veloutée qui déjà à Balbec dirigeait toutes mes journées vers le moment où, devant la mer mauve de septembre, je serais auprès de cette fleur rose, tentait douloureusement de s'unir un élément bien différent. Ce terrible besoin d'un être à Combray, j'avais appris à le connaître au sujet de ma mère, et jusqu'à vouloir mourir si elle me faisait dire par Françoise qu'elle ne pourrait pas monter. Cet effort de l'ancien sentiment pour se combiner et ne faire qu'un élément unique avec l'autre, plus récent, et qui, lui, n'avait pour voluptueux objet que la surface colorée, la rose carnation d'une fleur de plage, cet effort aboutit souvent à ne faire (au sens chimique) qu'un corps nouveau, qui peut ne durer que quelques instants. Ce soir-là, du moins, et pour longtemps encore, les deux éléments restèrent dissociés. (III, 130)

Furthermore, when his mother has no opinion about his relationship to Albertine, the narrator compares the decision about the commitment he must make to the responsibility he felt when his father gave him permission to see *Phèdre*. Both experiences ultimately mark the narrator's understanding of his own sexuality.

The superimposition of the narrator's mother and Albertine increases in intensity throughout the couple's relationship, and eventually Marcel's Pygmalion-like exploits seem to succeed. Usurping the mother's position in the family apartment while she is in Combray, the young woman treats the narrator with the same deference used by his mother and grandmother. Docility replaces the animation of Albertine's earliest Balbec days and the couple spends simple, relaxing evenings together during which they play checkers, his mistress entertains Marcel at the pianola or they enjoy quiet

---

to see *Phèdre*. The distinction seems to be between a play in which Mother-son incest occurs and one in which it does not. Even with Albertine the narrator explains that he was never her lover in the truest sense of the word (III, 604).

conversation. Albertine's intelligence, under her lover's tutelage, seems to measure up to the mother's and grandmother's and permits her the same appreciation of literature—Hardy, Dostoevsky and Stendhal. Most important, the anxiety the narrator once felt waiting for the mother's kiss reappears in his relationship with Albertine: "Qui m'eût dit à Combray . . . que ces anxiétés guériraient, puis renaîtraient un jour non pour ma mère, mais pour une jeune fille qui ne serait d'abord, sur l'horizon de la mer, qu'une fleur . . ." (IV, 82-83). The bedroom quickly becomes privileged space for the couple, the "point fixe et douloureux" (I, 9) of Marcel's preoccupation as it was in Combray and as it is when he writes his novel. Henceforth in the novel the two are rarely seen together anywhere else.

The "baiser maternel" quickly becomes a celebrated constant refrain and produces scenes which are obvious counterparts to many in Combray:

> Quand je pense maintenant que mon amie était venue . . . habiter à Paris sous le même toit que moi . . . et que chaque soir, fort tard, avant de me quitter, elle glissait dans ma bouche sa langue, comme un pain quotidien, comme un aliment nourrissant et ayant le caractère presque sacré de toute chair à qui les souffrances que nous avons endurées à cause d'elle ont fini par conférer une sorte de douceur morale, ce que j'évoque aussitôt par comparaison . . . [c'est] la nuit où mon père envoya maman dormir dans le petit lit à côté du mien. (III, 520)

Albertine's kiss has the same power to soothe, to console such as Marcel has not experienced since "les soirs lointains de Combray où ma mère penchée sur mon lit venait m'apporter le repos dans un baiser" (III, 585).

On the other hand, absence of Albertine's kiss excites the same anxiety. On the evenings he and his mistress quarrel, the narrator finds his feelings parallel those felt as a child when his mother, either angry or sometimes detained by guests, barely said good-night:

> comme si tous mes sentiments, qui tremblaient de ne pouvoir garder Albertine auprès de mon lit à la fois comme une maîtresse, comme une sœur, comme une fille, comme une mère aussi du bonsoir quotidien de laquelle je recommençais à éprouver le puéril besoin, avaient commencé de se rassembler, de s'unifier dans le soir prématuré de ma vie, qui semblait devoir être aussi brève qu'un jour d'hiver. (III, 619)

And finally eroticization of the "baiser maternel" occurs and becomes the very metaphor for the narrator's attempts to reconcile two contradictory ideas of femininity:

> sa langue maternelle, incomestible, nourricière et sainte, dont la flamme et la rosée secrètes faisaient que, même quand Albertine la faisait seulement glisser à la surface de mon cou, de mon ventre, ces caresses superficielles mais en quelque sorte faites par l'intérieur de sa chair, extériorisé comme une étoffe qui montrerait sa doublure, prenaient, même dans les attouchements les plus externes, comme la mystérieuse douceur d'une pénétration. (IV, 79)

Proust completes the collapse of Mother and Lover through use of the felicitous French homophones *mer/mère,* a technique others recognize as well. Bellemin-Noël plays on these same words in his analysis of Swann's dream: "D'autre part, le chemin où a lieu la promenade se rapproche et s'éloigne alternativement de la *mer:* chemin de bord de *mère,* tel que peut le parcourir toute première enfance . . ." (51). And Claudine Quémar praises Genette for having "pressenti le rôle primordial que jouent, dans la formation des images nominales chez Proust, les associations verbales fondées sur des homophonies ou des assonances" (81). In the case of Albertine "presque peinte sur le fond de la mer" (II, 656), she in reconstructed—like a house de *fond en comble*—on the foundation of the Mother. While the adolescent's appearance at the Normandy beach resort explains the constant comparison Albertine/mer, more significant is how—true to Proust's system à la Balzac—this outer landscape mirrors an inner one. In short, Proust's choice to place Albertine by the sea was not indiscriminate and initially he conflates all the young girls who, for the narrator, might each have become the beloved: ". . . je devrais plus encore donner un nom différent à chacune de ces Albertine qui apparaissaient devant moi, jamais la même, comme—appelées simplement par moi pour plus de commodité la mer . . ." (II, 299).

Interesting to note are the moments when Proust chooses to capitalize the word *mer.* It first occurs in Combray when the narrator discusses Balbec with Legrandin and the snob, himself a homosexual, seems to be subtly warning the boy against this landscape which, ostensibly synonymous with the Mother, may threaten the narrator's well-being: "Balbec! la plus antique ossature géologique de notre sol, vraiment Ar-mor [Amour?], la Mer, la fin de la terre, la région maudite qu'Anatole France . . . a si bien peinte . . ." (I, 129). Once in Balbec, Marcel personnifies the sea (her breathing, her smile, an invitation to walk beside her) that he eagerly admires every morning: "Mais avant tout j'avais ouvert mes rideaux dans l'impatience de savoir quelle était la Mer qui jouait ce matin-là au bord du rivage, comme une Néréide. Car chacune de ces Mers ne restait plus d'un jour" (II, 64-65).

But the most telling use of the capitalized Mer appears early in the text when the narrator is lost in contemplation of the *aubépines,* or hawthorns. They hold an indecipherable secret and Marcel turns away from the flowers hoping to return to them momentarily with fresh insight. Following a path behind the hedge, he sees a stray wild poppy that announces the fields that follow and makes his heart beat "comme au voyageur qui aperçoit sur une terre basse une première barque échouée que répare un calfat, et s'écrie, avant de l'avoir encore vue: 'La Mer!' " (I, 137). Directly on the heels of this exclamation, the narrator turns back to the hawthorns, commenting that "le sentiment qu'elles éveillaient . . . restait obscur et vague." While their significance remains as yet unrevealed to the narrator, the juxtaposition of *aubépine* with "La Mer!" is a crucial first clue to Marcel's sexuality and its link to the Mother. As Doubrovsky points out in *La Place de la madeleine,* Proust seems to exploit *pine,* the slang word for penis, and by adding to it the word *aube,* or dawn, signals Marcel's sexual awakening. Not surprisingly then, it is at this moment that the narrator first sees Gilberte, the girl who will initiate his love series founded on efforts to reconcile Mother and Lover and Albertine's most obvious predecessor.

Moreover, the rapprochement of Mother and Sea is evident in Marcel's pursuit of Mlle de Stermaria, a relationship which previews his efforts to reconcile Mother and Lover—and its outcome. Picturing the young woman on her Breton island the narrator imagines strolling alone with her "dans le crépuscule où luiraient plus doucement au-dessus de l'eau assombrie les fleurs roses des bruyères, sous les chênes battus par le clapotement des vagues" (II, 49). Later, visiting the Bois with Albertine where he has made arrangements to dine with Mlle de Stermaria and hoping to create a similar atmosphere, Marcel describes the location in marine terminology: "Nous fîmes quelques pas à pied, sous la grotte verdâtre, quasi sous-marine, d'une épaisse futaie sur le dôme de laquelle nous entendions déferler le vent et éclabousser la pluie. J'écrasais par terre des feuilles mortes qui s'enfonçaient dans le sol comme des coquillages et je poussais de ma canne des châtaignes, piquantes comme des oursins" (II, 683).

On the other hand, because the surname Stermaria is but a letter away from Ste Maria, the character's connection to the Mother is undeniable. Furthermore, it brings to mind an image in the Christian tradition which explicitly joins Mother and Sea: the Virgin Mary is frequently glorified as Stella Maris—Mary, Star of the Sea. Even more significant, Gilbert Durand points out in *Les Structures anthropologiques de l'imaginaire* that attraction to the sea or water, associated with the nocturnal as it is when Marcel pictures Mlle de Stermaria in her Breton environment, expresses a desire for the Mother and, more precisely, for the maternal womb: "La primordiale et suprême avaleuse est bien la mer . . . C'est l'abyssus féminisé et maternel qui pour de nombreuses cultures est l'archétype de la descente et du retour aux sources originelles du bonheur" (256).

Seen in this light, Albertine's sequestration results from Marcel's desire to repeat primary union, that moment beyond the womb that feels like the womb, a symbiosis necessarily limited to two and exclusive of all others. Fittingly then, *La Prisonnière* contains a spate of *mer/mère* parallels. No longer in Balbec, the narrator reflects: "Au reste, ce n'était pas seulement la mer à la fin de la journée qui vivait pour moi en Albertine, mais parfois l'assoupissement de la mer sur la grève par les nuits de clair de lune" (III, 577-78). The "mer à la fin de la journée" recalls, of course, the maternal kiss the hero normally received nightly as a child, and "l'assoupissement de la mer" suggests the calm, the lull in the narrator's anxiety that accompanied the goodnight kiss.

Significantly, this sentence opens the well known "la regarder dormir" passage in which the narrator describes his double pleasure, often onanistic, in simultaneously watching Albertine sleep and thinking about her leisurely and how he wishes. Consequently the narrator's efforts to impose the maternal role upon his mistress are unmistakable. The young woman but an inert body beside him, Marcel's phantasms are unfettered: ". . . je pouvais rêver à elle et pourtant la regarder, et quand ce sommeil devenait plus profond, la toucher, l'embrasser" (III, 578). Indeed, because his companion's eyes symbolize her fugitive life, once they are closed Marcel feels he can fill Albertine's emptied consciousness with his own and shape the young woman into the ideal beloved. Thus, it is no coincidence that the narrator imposes on his mistress the first dream associated with and loved in her—the mystery and allure of the *mer* which is, at the same time, the mystery and allure of the *mère*.

In this manner the narrator approaches what he considers a perfect state in love: "... sentant que son sommeil était dans son plein, et que je ne me heurterais pas à des écueils de conscience recouverts maintenant par la pleine mer du sommeil profond, délibérément je sautais sans bruit sur le lit . . . ." (III, 580). All doubts about Marcel's motives are dissipated when, following a description of his masturbatory pleasures, he adds: "Quelquefois on eût dit que la mer devenait grosse, que la tempête se faisait sentir jusque dans la baie, et je me mettais comme elle à écouter le grondement de son souffle qui ronflait" (III, 581). The marine imagery holds together beautifully. The high tide of Albertine's deep sleep turns into a heavy or high sea where a storm reverberates as far as the bay, and the narrator listens to the booming of the waves that is the young woman's snoring. However, it seems to me that Marcel's desire to transform Albertine into the ideal beloved, the Mother, permits another interpretation: "la grosse mer" becomes "la mère grosse," fecund lover, and resonates with the earlier "pleine mer/mère pleine." Both are the result of the "tempête [qui] se faisait sentir jusque dans la baie" which appears to be an orgasm reached in the opening that is the vagina.

Yet more important here than the seemingly oedipal superimposition of Mother and Lover is the narrator's preoedipal search for primary union which inspires it. Indeed, it seems that the *scène du coucher* makes such a remarkable impression that it is easy to overlook what a small role the mother—rather than the Mother—plays. However, using object relations theory, Dorothy Dinnerstein pursues the implications of this phenomenon and places the quest for the primary caretaker, the initial provider of contact with humanity and nature, at the root of all adult relationships:

> A woman is the witness in whose awareness the child's existence is first mirrored and confirmed, the audience who celebrates its earliest acts of achievement. This woman, moreover, is the overwhelming external will in the face of which the child first learns the necessity for submission, the first being to whose wishes the child may be forced by punishment to subordinate its own, the first powerful and loved creature whom the child tries voluntarily to please. She is, in addition, the

person around whom the peculiarly ambiguous human attitude toward the flesh begins to be formed. It is in the relation with her that the child experiences the earliest version of what will be a lifelong internal conflict: the conflict between our rootedness in the body's acute, narrow joys and vicissitudes and our commitment to large-scale human concerns. (Dinnerstein 28-29)

Underscoring three fundamental characteristics of adult sexual relationships, Dinnerstein's observations correspond revealingly to the narrator's intimate life with Albertine. First of all, the desire for oneness with the Mother privileges a sexual asymmetry based on the male notion that "attachment to a woman is emotionally bearable, consistent with the solidarity among men which is part of maleness, only if she, and one's feelings toward her, remain under safe control" (50). Thus, points out Dinnerstein, while men need not be faithful, *they must have exclusive access to a woman*. In Marcel's case, not only does Albertine's sequestration (". . . je l'avais cachée à tout le monde . . ." [III, 519]) forcefully demonstrate the lover's need for sole possession of his partner, but of course, the narrator's relationship with his mother is its model.

Furthermore, Dinnerstein uses the vocabulary of imprisonment when expanding upon the reasons for exclusiveness. Men, she observes, wish to keep female will "in live captivity, obediently energetic, fiercely protective of its captor's pride" (169) so that it might galvanize male efforts, whatever they may be, with magical maternal approval and support them with self-sacrificing maternal help. The woman finds herself in a double-bind which requires her to assume these maternal responsibilities but also infantile helplessness. Albertine, after all, cannot go anywhere unchaperoned. The man, however, reaps a double benefit: Mother is under control and her power put to male profit while the man has no moral obligation. In Marcel's case, there is never any urgent sense that, as long as Albertine is his prisoner, he will in fact marry her. Ultimately though, holding a woman captive allows men, certainly Marcel, to act out a fantasy of taking care of mamma (". . . garder Albertine auprès de mon lit à la fois comme une maîtresse, comme une sœur, comme une fille, comme une mère . . ." [III, 619]), resulting from both gratitude and hostility, and which reverses the balance of power.

Indeed, secondly men must control their partner's independent sexual impulsivity, feared because it brings to mind the terrifying erotic independence of every baby's mother. The narrator also illustrates this attitude superbly for it is literally his fear of what Albertine's true sexuality might be that prompts him to keep her prisoner. Having discovered that Albertine, friend of Mlle Vinteuil's companion, hopes to see her in Trieste, Marcel admits, "pour qu'Albertine n'allât pas à Trieste . . . je l'aurais isolée, enfermée, je lui eusse pris le peu d'argent qu'elle avait pour que le dénuement l'empêchât matériellement de faire le voyage" (III, 505). But, the narrator discovers, returning to his apartment with a bouquet of seringas, even keeping her captive in Paris doesn't ensure that his mistress's sexual impulses are under control: "Elle avait failli être surprise avec Andrée, et s'était donné un peu de temps en éteignant tout, en allant chez moi pour ne pas laisser voir son lit en désordre . . ." (III, 564).

Finally, not wanting to become too much the baby, men distance themselves from their partner and sexual excitement is less intimately tied to personal sentiment. Again the narrator serves as an excellent illustration. The "la regarder dormir" passage proves that Marcel's most erotic moments occur when his mistress, while present, is a nonparticipant in his sexual excitement. A love object in the truest sense, Albertine does nothing but lie there and inspire his gaze. In short, although many may wish to use Proust's homosexuality to explain this characterization, the couple never really connects (so to speak). During her waking hours as well Marcel is careful to keep her in her place—that is to say at a distance—to maintain his own emotional equilibrium, even feigning that they separate: ". . . il vaut mieux nous quitter, et comme les séparations les meilleures sont celles qui s'effectuent le plus rapidement, je vous demande, pour abréger le grand chagrin que je vais avoir, de me dire adieu ce soir . . ." (III, 844).

Inevitably this preoedipally marked return-to-oneness-with-Mother synonymous with the adult sexual relationship reproduces, understandably, the ambivalence of the child constrained too long in this first developmental stage. That the Mother is perceived as synonymous with Nature—global, inchoate and all-embracing—exacerbates this emotional polarity. The narrator makes unequivocally clear the Mother/Lover=Nature equation when he comments: "Mais si ce désir qu'une femme apparût ajoutait pour moi aux charmes de la nature quelque chose de plus exaltant, les charmes de la nature, en retour, élargissaient ce que celui de la femme aurait eu de trop restreint" (I, 154). Like Nature, the Mother becomes the ultimate source of good and evil, and this notion, Dinnerstein feels, underlies human unease with both Nature and sexual arrangements. Consequently, whether in the face of Nature, Woman or Mother there is the contradictory wish "to own, control, suck dry the source of good . . . and the impulse, on the other hand, to make reparation for these feelings, which threaten to destroy what is most precious and deeply needed" (100).

The Proustian dichotomy seemingly equates the good mother with Nature while categorizing the bad mother as unnatural. However, the object-splitting this system represents signals the fact that these mothers are one in the same. She is both good and evil. And Marcel, confronting Nature, Woman or Mother, displays this conflicted behavior Dinnerstein describes. He wishes to devour Nature: standing before lilacs during a Tansonville walk he speaks of his "désir d'enlacer leur taille souple et d'attirer à moi les boucles étoilées de leur tête odorante . . ." (I, 134); Woman: the narrator's jealousy is the symptom of his inability to know completely, to possess through exhaustive knowledge, Albertine; and the Mother: of his grandmother Marcel says, "Quand j'avais ainsi ma bouche collée à ses joues, à son front, j'y puisais quelque chose de si bienfaisant, de si nourricier, que je gardais l'immobilité, le sérieux, la tranquille avidité d'un enfant qui tète" (II, 28). To make amends Marcel appears to place Nature on a pedestal, plies his mistress with expensive gifts and a promise of marriage, and resuscitates in his novel the memory of his grandmother, whom he felt (as did Proust of his own mother) he had depleted of life.

Furthermore, this analogy between Woman and Nature strips females of their subjectivity. Overpersonification of Nature makes it appear somewhat sentient while underpersonification of Woman makes her seem less than human. Thus a return to oneness with the Mother also becomes a menace to selfhood. Woman is the original non-self, both it and you, which threatens formation of the I and who can always lure others back into non-being "to engulf, dissolve, drown, suffocate them as autonomous persons" (Dinnerstein 112). Indeed, Michael Balint describes union with the Mother as an oceanic feeling, and moreover, in this adult quest for merger, the woman becomes phylogenetically the all-embracing sea (Chodorow 194). Thus, Marcel appropriately compares Albertine to "une pierre qui enferme la salure des océans immémoriaux" (III, 888), and Proust's conflation of the *mère/mer* becomes all the more meaningful. Of the 944 images which have their source in Nature in *La Recherche,* 326 of these are taken from water and the sea (Graham 119). On the one hand, blissful union with the Mother, whether the narrator's mother or Albertine, seems to be Marcel's goal, and yet on the other hand, because they are synonymous with the sea, he seems to struggle to set himself free of both in order to establish finally his autonomous self.

To do this the narrator will write his novel because the ultimate ambivalence towards women lies in the relationship between carnality, mortality and enterprise. Human resentment of the body's mortality is aimed particularly against the Mother, for the flesh from which all individuals emerge also tells them they will die. Renunciation of this original body results and pleasure-giving and death-defying enterprise replace it:

> In sum, human ambivalence toward the body of woman arises from, and at the same time helps perpetuate, incompetence to reconcile our inevitable mix of feelings for the flesh itself. The unreconciled mix is projected onto the first parent. Worse still, much of the positive side of this ambivalence is suppressed and what has been suppressed is converted into an obscene preoccupation; this means that even the love that is part of the prevailing attitude toward woman's body is to some degree a dirty love. The shame that for many people tinges carnal attraction is made possible by, and at the same time deepens, women's general human degradation . . . Both this failure to integrate our feelings toward the flesh and this debasement of what is positive in these feelings express our helplessness to cope with carnality, a helplessness that has so far permeated the death-denying, and therefore death-dominated, life of our enterprising species. Women's status as scapegoat-idol is maintained by, and at the same time works to maintain, this helplessness. (Dinnerstein 148)

As for Marcel, he will create himself by engaging in an enterprise which escapes the flesh and thus death. More important, it will free him from the Mother.

But what moves the narrator to this realization is the discovery, first of all, that primary union with the Mother is impossible if for no other reason than it is never one of seamless mutuality. Whereas the boy Marcel's need for his mother was absolute, her need for him was relative. From time to time, her interest was focused on other people, her husband, or other activities, such as dinner with Swann. Proust himself understood this only too well, for Jeanne Proust's attentions were often diverted to his younger brother Robert. While Painter uses aesthetic reasons to explain this neglect, the sibling's total absence from the novel bears witness to how traumatic this was. Dinnerstein even suggests that male infidelity is a way of punishing the Mother for these dalliances. Thus, when the narrator falls in love with Albertine, he must confront, because adult love comes second, the object relations that bind both partners to the Mother and, as a result, the notion—already suggested in his relationship with the primary caretaker— that his partner has separate needs and a separate viewpoint never completely subject to his own.

Nothing makes this phenomenon clearer to the narrator than his inability to comprehend Albertine's sexuality. Proust builds Albertine's lesbianism discreetly, noting that Gomorrha is a puzzle that one puts together with pieces from the most unexpected places (III, 597)—and its increasing evidence corresponds directly to Marcel's decreasing poetization of love which leads to the elaboration of his novel. First suggested by the Andrée/Albertine waltz, Albertine's preference for females instinctively strikes the narrator again when he accuses her of lying. His companion answers that she will never see him again: "La mer sera mon tombeau. Je ne vous reverrai jamais . . . Je me noierai . . ." (III, 197). Within the context of the *mer/mère* homonymy this is a loaded response and implies that the Mother will cause the narrator's loss of Albertine. The narrator immediately replies, "Comme Sapho." Of course, legend has it that the Lesbos poet did indeed throw herself into the sea. But the convergence, in this case, of motherhood and lesbianism captured by *mer* becomes even more of a possibility in the narrator's mind when he discovers that Mlle Vinteuil's lesbian companion also served as a surrogate mother for his mistress: "Vous vous rappelez que je vous ai parlé d'une amie plus âgée que moi qui m'a servi de mère, de sœur . . . et que d'ailleurs je dois dans quelques semaines retrouver à Cherbourg, d'où nous voyagerons ensemble (c'est un peu baroque, mais vous savez comme j'aime la mer) . . ." (III, 499). It is well known that this moment is also the crystalization of the narrator's love and what compels him to keep the woman a virtual prisoner in Paris, with Andrée as her constant companion.

However, Mlle Vinteuil's friend and Andrée both are ultimately responsible for the break between Marcel and Albertine. In the first case, Marcel insists that his companion not visit Mme Verdurin for fear that she might meet the lesbian couple. This leads to a repetition of the Combray scene in which the narrator asks Françoise to interrupt his parents' dinner with Swann by delivering a note soliciting his mother's presence in his room. Now Marcel tries to keep Albertine away from Mlle Vinteuil and her companion by sending her to the theatre only to find that the quintessential lesbian Léa will be performing. The narrator sends Françoise off to Trocadéro with a note meant to bring his mistress back. However, the very significant difference between the two scenes is that in the first the narrator competes with another male for the beloved's attention, and in the second, he competes with a female. But, in fact, the female rival is double. It is not just Léa but potentially Mlle Vinteuil and her companion, tripling the female competition. Ultimately it quadruples because of the ubiquitous Andrée, and indeed, she becomes the second prominent reason for the couple's separation when Marcel renews his accusations about the Andrée/Albertine relationship.

Moreover, while the first Françoise/note scene leads to the pivotal *scène du coucher* that marks the beginning of Marcel's quest for primary union, the later scene leads to the narrator's discovery that this search will ultimately exclude him. When for the first time during their Paris living arrangement Albertine refuses Marcel the maternal kiss ("Quand elle vint me dire bonsoir et que je l'embrassai . . . elle ne me rendit pas mon baiser" [III, 900]), the young woman seems to be telling her companion that she will refuse to play the maternal role if he denies her her lesbian pursuits.

It seems to me that this gives new meaning to the narrator's love series. While it is true that every woman he loves shares a resemblance through her link to the Mother, to my mind, what makes the Mother unequivocally the source of this *série amoureuse* is her role as love object for women as well. Any woman the narrator loves may potentially seek other women. Thus the love series metamorphoses into an ever growing number of women who do not increase the number of love objects for the narrator, but rather for one another. That is why throughout the novel Albertine is never legitimately pictured with another male. There is a brief flirtation with Saint-Loup during a seaside train ride, Mme Verdurin's interest in marrying the young woman to her nephew Octave, and Albertine's tie to Morel. But in truth, even these tenuous connections are of little merit because, in contrast to Swann, all these men are linked to homosexuality. Furthermore, faced with Albertine's possible lesbianism, the narrator never does what he feels compelled to do for homosexuality. Never does he pass in review all the *idées reçues* on female inversion, but instead, Marcel investigates Albertine "under the category of 'the beloved object' or, *as if this were synonymous, simply of 'woman'*" (Sedgwick 232—emphasis added). In short, for Proust lesbianism is the very essence of the female, powerful for its very inability to be known.

Marcel suspects as much and tries to imagine, following Albertine's death, the young woman's relations:

> Et certes c'était déjà un commencement de souffrance que de me la représenter désirant comme j'avais si souvent désiré, me mentant comme je lui avais si souvent menti, préoccupée par telle ou telle jeune fille, faisant des frais pour elle, comme moi pour Mlle de Stermaria, pour tant d'autres, ou pour les paysannes que je rencontrais dans la campagne. (IV, 98)

Andrée confirms Marcel's suspicions: ". . . maintenant qu'Andrée avouait ces goûts, la conclusion qui devait s'imposer à mon esprit était qu'Albertine et Andrée avaient toujours eu des relations ensemble" (IV, 127-28). Indeed, the narrator understands how Andrée has filled the maternal role and sees how the mediation of mother and lover actually takes place unexpectedly within the lesbian woman, necessarily eliminating the narrator.

Marcel sees motherhood now, not only as an obstacle to mutual love but that which makes love between the sexes impossible: ". . . derrière la plage de Balbec, *la mer* . . . je voyais, avec des mouvements de désespoir . . . *la chambre de Montjouvain* où Albertine . . . avait pris la place de l'amie de Mlle Vinteuil . . . C'est *cette scène* que je voyais derrière celle qui s'étendait dans la fenêtre et *qui n'était sur l'autre qu'un voile morne, superposé comme un reflet*" (III, 513-14—emphasis added).

This confusion of motherhood and lesbianism is in fact suggested in Combray. As Florival points out, the "mois de Marie" hawthorn bushes the boy Marcel sees walking to Tansonville with his father and grandfather reflect in their freshness the cheeks of Mlle Vinteuil (I,112), known for her robust health. In this manner Proust subtly insinuates a relationship between venerated motherhood and the most denegrated of feminine activities. Moreover, by placing side by side the Holy Mother and the best known lesbian of his novel, he capsulizes the progression his work will take: ostensibly an adoration of Mother, it metamorphoses into her rejection. The narrator does not—as Bersani sees it—pursue lesbians, women indifferent to men, as a form of self-punishment for sins of exaggerated possessiveness against the mother and selfish indifference against the grandmother. Instead, Marcel discovers within lesbians the futility of pursuing the Mother and decides not to punish himself but to punish *her*. Painter sees Proust's cruelty as compensation for the injustice of having to share Jeanne Proust's love with Robert. But, in truth, punishment is exacted for selfish indifference (the asymmetry of their relationship) as well as for the sins of exaggerated possessiveness (the suffocatingly long preoedipal):

> Albertine . . . était entrée pour moi dans cette période lamentable où un être, disséminé dans l'espace et dans le temps, n'est plus pour nous une femme, mais une suite d'événements sur lesquels nous ne pouvons faire la lumière, une suite de problèmes insolubles, *une mer que nous essayons ridiculement,* comme Xerxès, *de battre pour la punir de ce qu'elle a englouti.* (III, 612—emphasis added)

Thus, Marcel's failure to reconcile two definitions of femininity and attendant failure to achieve mutual love see the Mother as responsible. Henceforth, this role, seen so favorably in Combray but already deteriorating seriously during Marcel's relationship with Albertine, becomes progressively aberrant. The *mer/mère*, "Matrice universelle . . . [qui] est bien le champ premier, la structure ontologique du monde . . ." (Florival 63), is also the matrix and mould, uterus and womb, that is to say, the place par excellence of promise from which this repudiation of motherhood bodies forth. His novel will be a painful but therapeutic return to the source that will allow him to revisit the past and also to put it behind him: "S'il est vrai que la mer ait été autrefois notre milieu vital où il faille replonger notre sang pour retrouver nos forces, il en est de même de l'oubli, du néant mental . . ." (II, 178).

Chapter Four

Mothers and Daughters: The Lesbian Continuum

In the "I'll-be-the-mamma-you-be-the-baby" scenario of Dinnerstein's adult sexual relations the woman doesn't simply assume the maternal role but plays the child as well. She, too, is looking for the Mother. But, Chodorow points out, this leads Freud to an interesting contradiction. He observes that people who choose an anaclitic love object choose someone modeled on the Mother and opposite to the self. In contrast, those who choose a narcissistic love object choose someone modeled on the self. While the psychoanalyst considers anaclitic love to be complete object love for both genders he, nonetheless, expects women to take men for a love object. *A la recherche du temps perdu* illustrates the folly of this expectation.

Indeed, the novel contains an extraordinary number of women loving women. Moreover, they appear to respect a nineteenth-century literary tradition that not only provides numerous androgynes and lesbians but also leaves them motherless. *Mlle de Maupin* is the best example but there are others such as Philip Cuisine's *Clémentine, Orpheline et Androgyne,* 1819; Henri de la Touche's *Fragoletta,* 1829; Rachilde's *Monsieur Vénus,* 1884; Pierre Louijs's *Aphrodite,* 1896 in addition to Colette's *Claudine à l'école* published in 1900. Proust both cites works from this group—Barbey d'Aurevilly's *Les Diaboliques* ("Le rideau cramoisi") and Balzac's *La Fille aux yeux d'or*—and peoples his own text with several orphans. Among these are, of course, Mlle Vinteuil and Albertine but also Oriane de Guermantes, raised by Mme de Villeparisis, and Bloch's sisters or even Odette who had been abandoned by her mother.

Furthermore, Proustian females who merit the label motherless because their mothers, "mères méchantes," abuse the maternal role turn to lesbianism as well. Andrée and Gilberte, whose mothers are caught up in self-interest, are implicated in homosexual relationships: Andrée in her intimate friendship with Albertine and, later, Gilberte who is seen walking the Champs-Elysées with the known lesbian actress Léa. Ultimately it seems that virtually all Proust's female characters from major to minor, from Mme Verdurin to the Princesse de Parme (who shares a curious conversation with Oriane about the duchess's celebrated hermaphroditic orchids), are labeled lesbians, and that the only women who escape this category are the unquestionably good mothers, the narrator's grandmother and mother, Françoise and Mme Cottard. Even the editors of Volume IV of *La Recherche*'s new edition feel obliged to make this observation. Commenting on a textual variation which reveals, in a conversation between Andrée and the narrator after Albertine's death, Mme Bontemps's sexual relations with her niece, they remark: "Dans cet ajout tardif, qui ne fut pas inséré, Mme Bontemps entre elle aussi dans Gomorrhe: il semble que moins pour les besoins du récit . . . que pour le simple plaisir d'y rattacher toute la gent féminine du roman" (IV, 652).

Proust's own homosexuality can easily explain the presence of several homosexual males in his novel, but this astonishing number of homosexual women warrants an explanation. Here, I think the author's essay "A propos de Baudelaire" suggests some interesting possibilities. Writing about Alfred de Vigny as well as Baudelaire, to his mind the two greatest nineteenth-century poets, Proust notes that Vigny imbued "La Colère de Samson" with intensity through jealousy in his own life over friendships that his lover Marie Dorval had with other women. In fact within *La Recherche* itself Swann ruminates over lines from Vigny's *Journal d'un poète* when contemplating Odette's potential lesbianism, finding particularly pertinent Vigny's suggestion that a man in love needs to look at the people around his beloved and ask himself what her former life was like. The "Samson" poem, however, fascinates Proust, not for its advice to the lover, but by its portrait of femininity. Woman is reduced to the mysteries of the breast: "il rêvera toujours à la chaleur du sein"; to physiological peculiarity: "la femme, enfant malade et douze fois impur"; and to psychological treachery: "toujours ce compagnon dont le coeur n'est pas sûr." Thus, it is understandable, says Proust, that Vigny should have

Mothers and Daughters: The Lesbian Continuum 59

opposed men and women as irreconcilable enemies: "La femme aura Gomorrhe et l'homme aura Sodome." Uncomfortable with Baudelaire's self-assigned role of interpreter in "Lesbos" ("Car Lesbos entre tous m'a choisi sur la terre / Pour chanter le secret de ces vierges en fleurs / Et je fus dès l'enfance admis au noir mystère."), Proust is much more at ease with Vigny's compulsion to separate the sexes, using, as he does, the Vigny poem as an epigraph for *Sodome et Gomorrhe,* a choice made five years earlier as Proust explained in a 1920 letter to the well known lesbian Natalie Clifford Barney.

More significant though is the manner in which the poet's unflattering picture of womanhood corresponds precisely to the infelicitous Proustian image. Obviously the author of *La Recherche* believes just as firmly as does Vigny that women are inconstant and chronically incapable of unflagging devotion. And while Proust does not literally depict the female body as the contaminated and practically untouchable human flesh that Vigny describes, his reticence with regard to the female body, and the veiled manner in which he finally does discuss it when he describes Albertine, suggests at the very least unease: "Les deux petits seins haut remontés étaient si ronds qu'ils avaient moins l'air de faire partie intégrante de son corps que d'y avoir mûri comme deux fruits; et son ventre . . . se refermait, à la jonction des cuisses, par deux valves . . ." (III, 587).

These are the same valves which Proust uses to describe the madeleine, and because, as Doubrovsky explains, the small cake represents the Mother, they reinforce the first of Vigny's three complaints, the reproach which is most telling. Representing the female metonymically as breast, the anatomical part that best symbolizes nurturance of the child, the poet[1] seems to suggest along with Proust that motherhood is the obstacle which keeps the two sexes segregated. In fact, the title of Dinnerstein's study which sees the Mother as source of the malaise in adult sexual relations captures this very same adversarial division. On the one hand, there is the mermaid, "treacherous . . . seductive and impenetrable female representation of the dark and magic underwater world from which our life comes

---

[1] Later Proust uses Leconte de Lisle's "Hymne orphique" to reinforce the same Mother/Lover connection: "Or ces désirs pour une femme dont on a rêvé ne rendent pas absolument nécessaire la beauté de tel trait précis. Ces désirs sont seulement le désir de tel être . . . l'encens le parfum de la mère (III, 234).

and in which it cannot live," and on the other hand, the minotaur, "fearsome ... gigantic and eternally infantile offspring of a mother's unnatural lust, male representative of mindless, greedy power, [who] insatiably devours live human flesh" (5). Not coincidentally, Proust's text adheres to this symbolism. Certainly the Sea/Mother equation is exceedingly prominent and the minotaur appears obliquely through references to *Phèdre,* dramatic paradigm for the narrator's negative experience of love. Reflecting on the scene in which the heroïne declares her love for Hippolytus, Marcel comments: "Il me semblait que ce que je m'étais si souvent récité à moi-même et que j'avais écouté au théâtre, c'était l'énoncé des lois que je devais expérimenter dans ma vie" (IV, 41).

However, the mutual love missing between Mother/Lover/Phaedra and Hippolytus, like that of Albertine and Marcel, not only finds its origin in the Mother but, as the Albertine/Mlle Vinteuil's companion connection implies, in the relationship between Mother and Daughter. Proust appears obsessed with what Irigaray calls "le continent noir du continent noir" (1981, 61). Indeed, even Freud, originator of the dark continent notion, felt that women could not be understood without an appreciation of their preoedipal attachment to the Mother. In his "Femininity" lecture the psychoanalyst obseves:

> We know, of course, that there had been a preliminary stage of attachment to the mother, but we did not know that it could be so rich in content and so long-lasting, and could leave behind so many opportunities for fixations and dispositions ... Almost everything that we find later in her relation to her father was already present in this earlier attachment and has been transferred subsequently on to her father. In short, we get an impression that we cannot understand women unless we appreciate this phase of their pre-Oedipus attachment to their mother. (119)

In order to understand the implications of this observation for lesbians in *La Recherche*—and ultimately for the narrator as well—a few additional comments about the preoedipal are necessary. Primacy of this period, which lasts in girls until age four or five and is, consequently, extremely intense and ambivalent, has significant repercussions in an adult woman's sexual arrangements. It both determines her oedipal attachment to her father and, in turn, her later relationship to men in general. As Chodorow demonstrates, when girls reach the oedipal phase they do not simply transfer affection from the mother to the father, but instead, because of the continual importance of external and internal relations to the mother, they *add* the father to the mother-daughter dyad (92-93). And the daughter's attachment to the mother continues to concern itself with early mother-infant relational issues of dependence and individuation. Females come to experience themselves as less separate than males, with more permeable ego boundaries much as Irigaray describes them in *L'Une ne bouge pas sans l'autre*.

Nonetheless, while maternal influence is extraordinary in female development, the outcome of the oedipal period for most girls is heterosexuality. (Freud cites three oedipal tasks: the father replaces the mother as the girl's love object; the libidinal mode changes from active to passive; and the vagina replaces the clitoris as the libidinal organ.) Moreover, Chodorow underscores this very merging of mother and daughter as the essential reason for their heterosexual orientation: "When an omnipotent mother perpetuates primary love and primary identification in relation to her daughter, and creates boundaries and a differentiated, anaclitic love relation to her son, a girl's father is likely to become a symbol of freedom from this dependence and merging" (121). Furthermore, to justify rejection of the mother, the female projects all the good object qualities of the internalized mother image and the inner relationship to her onto the father as external object and onto her relationship with him, while transferring all the bad elements of the father image to the mother. Gilberte's relationship to Swann illustrates this very nicely. Initially the girl had no paternal presence whatsoever because Odette, as yet unmarried to Swann, refused to let him see his daughter until he made such a commitment. The reader is left to assume that what is normally a close mother/child union is unrelievedly so in the Odette/Gilberte relationship. Thus, when Odette and Swann finally wed, this male presence is a welcome escape, and in fact, Swann is pictured as a doting father. Gilberte is devoted to him as a young woman, and the narrator observes that her temperament, which vacillates between paternal and maternal characteristics, is more congenial when the balance swings toward her father's personality.

The upshot of all this—and it is the common psychoanalytic view—is that the female Oedipus Complex is as much a function of a girl's relationship to her mother as it is to her father; maternal primacy in the oedipal situation is as important for females as it is for males. This leads to a significant difference in oedipal resolution. While the boy usually chooses the mother as love object and represses this desire through fear of castration, the daughter, who does not have this same fear, feels free to keep both mother and father as love objects. And because her attachment to the father is not as exclusive and comes later than the boy's attachment to the mother, the father-daughter relationship never has the intensity of the mother-son union.

More significant, Chodorow replaces mother-son incest, normally seen as the most potentially regressive relationship, with mother-daughter incest. She is speaking not necessarily about consummated relationships but rather about those that are sufficiently involved emotionally or libidinally to prevent the daughter from having an extrafamilial sexual relationship: "Mother-daughter incest may be the most 'socially regressive,' in the sense of a basic threat to species survival, since a mother and son can at least produce a child" (132). Irigaray says virtually the same thing: "La relation mère/fille, fille/mère constitue un noyau extrêmement explosif dans nos sociétés. La penser, la changer, revient à ébranler l'ordre patriarcal" (1981, 86).

Finally, the assumption that heterosexual orientation is biologically normal and woman's biological destiny is shaky. Schafer points out in "Problems in Freud's Psychology" that this notion is anchored in a societal value system based in taken for granted evolutionary obligations, not in value free empiricism (471). In addition, psychoanalytic clinical findings evidence nothing ineluctable, natural or preestablished in the development of human sexuality. The opposite appears true. Cases demonstrate that sexual orientation and definition are constructed and enforced by parents, a phenomenon seemingly of particular importance to females in the mother-dominant/father-absent world. (However, Chodorow notes, there is no evidence that paternal absence correlates with female homosexuality [175].) Thus it is possible, says Chodorow, to accept the psychoanalytic account which delineates the genesis of heterosexual orientation in women and reject any idea that it is natural at the same time: "To the contrary, it seems to be both consciously and unconsciously intended, socially, psychologically, and ideologically constructed" (113).

It seems to me, then, that the number of mothers and daughters in *La Recherche* and the way they overwhelm the mother-son relationship is significant. Indeed, there is only one prominent mother-son couple—the narrator and his mother. Certainly there is the Mme de Marsantes/Saint-Loup pair but she appears relatively rarely in the text and they appear even less frequently as mother and son. There is Charlus and his mother who has apparently marked him indelibly and so much so that it is easy to forget that she was also mother to the Duc de Guermantes. But she is dead before the novel begins. Among the lesser characters Mme Cottard has a son, but he never appears in the text. And among the very minor are Mme de Surgis and her sons Arnolphe and Victurnien.

Mothers and daughters, on the other hand, are exceedingly numerous and, of course, among them the narrator's grandmother and mother are unquestionably the most important. In addition, there are Odette and Gilberte, Gilberte and Mlle de Saint-Loup, Françoise and her daughter as well as Andrée and her mother. Among those women with secondary roles are Tante Léonie and her mother, the narrator's great aunt, and the actress Berma and her daughter. There are also those women who, because they lack biological mothers, have surrogates. Mme de Villeparisis serves as the Duchesse de Guermantes's mother. Mme Bontemps is Albertine's, but according to the young woman, she has an additional mother in Mlle Vinteuil's companion, who possibly plays this role for the composer's daughter as well. Odette finds a surrogate mother in Mme Verdurin. Finally, there is the extratextual and positive paradigmatic mother-daughter dyad of Mme de Sévigné and Mme de Grignan.

Moreover, these mother-daughter connections are so powerful that they illustrate Robert Stoller's observation that, because primary identity for boys and girls alike is female, females are probably stronger. What he calls their "homosexuality" may give them an advantage. Developing unshakeable links with the mother's femaleness and femininity in normal mother-child symbiosis augments a girl's identity. "If a mother can lay down *that* foundation in her daughter, then a strength—a permanence, a part of identity—is well situated and can serve the child even in the face of later adversities, as in the oedipal situation" (359). Furthermore, Irigaray uses the mirror or *glace* as sign of mother/daughter interpenetration because it reflects, literally, the similarity of the two females but also because its double meaning captures, perhaps literally as well, the younger woman's feeling of being paralyzed within the first. Proust is unequivocal about the caretaker's influence: ". . . il suffisait de voir à côté de ces jeunes filles leur mère ou leur tante, pour mesurer les distances que sous l'attraction interne d'un type généralement affreux, ces traits auraient traversées dans moins de trente ans . . ." (II, 245). Oriane ultimately finds herself as *déclassée* as Mme de Villeparisis; like Mme Bontemps Albertine becomes *hommasse;* and Gilberte realizes, when the narrator sees her at the Princesse de Guermantes's (Mme Verdurin's) reception that he mistakes her for Odette. But, in addition, the author inadvertently suggests, when Albertine freely sizes up two of Léa's companions by looking in a strategically placed mirror, the potential for mother/daughter fusion to expand into the lesbian couple— something which all three of these women supposedly do. In fact, this Proustian female network is so marked that it captures what Adrienne Rich terms the lesbian continuum, that which, while not eliminating the sexual, emphasizes shared female experience.

At first glance many of these relationships might appear too adversarial to suggest any mutual understanding among women. And yet, whether amicable or acrimonious, their relations are anchored in a female economy. These are women-identified women. Mediation illustrates, for example, that the feminine identification process is always in relationship to another woman. Oriane de Guermantes wishes to reign in the Faubourg Saint-Germain, not to please the duke or any other male, but to be the most valued female among other *haut monde* females. In addition, rather than distancing herself from her husband's mistresses, she systematically turns each into "une précieuse alliée" (II, 771). When Mme Verdurin marries the Prince de Guermantes, it is obviously not for love, even money really, but to alert all those women who formerly rejected her that now she holds sway over them. The deceased Princesse de Guermantes, by virtue of her startling replacement, is in greater evidence than the prince. And the disloyalty of Berma's daughter occurs when she pays hommage to another woman, the actress Rachel. Moreover, the traditional construct in which the husband/father formally articulates family status in society is stood on its head. Whether Tante Léonie in Combray, Oriane in the Faubourg Saint-Germain, or Mme Verdurin cum Princesse de Guermantes, a woman is the axis around which all else revolves, the standard by which everyone is measured.

Furthermore, because the mother remains a daughter's primary internal object and though most women emerge from the Oedipus Complex erotically heterosexual, heterosexual love and emotional commitment are less exclusively established. In short, men tend to remain emotionally secondary, a phenomenon that the women of *La Recherche* demonstrate superbly. Queen of Combray, Tante Léonie's greatest fear is that her dead husband Octave will be resuscitated. Françoise would not lift a finger for her son-in-law but would walk miles for her daughter in need. As long as she is comfortably settled in high society, Gilberte will allow Saint-Loup his extramarital activities, straight or gay. Men simply do not represent the intensity and exclusiveness that women represent to men as the contrast between Albertine and Marcel surely makes clear. They have, Chodorow notes, a richer, ongoing inner world to fall back on, a phenomenon that Tante Léonie makes comically evident! Moreover, women retain and develop a greater number of relationships, as the salon circuit demonstrates, and developmentally men do not become as emotionally important to women as women do to men (198). Vinteuil's influence on the psychic development of his daughter seems negligible whereas the narrator's mother's influence is fundamental to his psychic development.

Most important in this lesbian continuum, though, is how heterosexual relations are simply one woman's search for another woman, the Mother. In love-making, women, like men, wish to compensate for loss of the Mother, and both sexes do so first hand by taking bodily pleasure and second hand by providing bodily pleasure. However, the male can more easily relive infant experience, quite simply, because his female partner's body resembles the Mother's. For females, then, the more prominent role is the vicarious one in which her own sexual impulsivity is constrained since it brings to everyone's mind the menacing erotic independence of the baby's mother.[2]

In addition, during love-making the woman is more apt to put herself in the man's place in order to meet her partner's needs rather than pursue her desire. Less engrossed in her own access to his body, she simultaneously attenuates her own access to the Mother and emphasizes instead her maternal role of caretaker and nurturer. Ironically, it is the permeable boundaries typical of the mother-daughter dyad that permit her to merge more easily with the personality of the person to whose flesh she is drawn.

---

[2] Christiane Olivier, a psychoanalyst, comments that her male patients complain with great frequency that their partners have their own desires and find it outrageous that a woman should wish to exist in any other way than how they have willed it (64).

Consequently, added to the contradiction between freedom of male sexuality and tightly controlled female sexuality is the disparity between female carnal excitement grounded in personal sentiment and male carnal excitement, anchored in the heteroerotic mother-son relationship, which has no need for such support.

Finally, because of the child's original, monolithic wish for the Mother and the notion that this need is acceptable only if male feelings are carefully monitored, the woman must be faithful to one man. On the other hand, rarely can she count on male fidelity, and the man might even choose a man-sharing situation in which his partner is obliged to share him with another woman. However, this does hold some advantages for the woman. Excited by her partner's access to another female body, *she* also has reaccess to a female erotic figure, but, once again, vicariously. In fact, Albertine seems to resolve this problem, or at least tries, by finding a male partner who resembles a female friend. The narrator remarks: "A ce moment je m'aperçus dans la glace; je fus frappé d'une certaine ressemblance entre moi et Andrée. Si je n'avais pas cessé depuis longtemps de raser ma moustache et si je n'en avais eu qu'une ombre, cette ressemblance eût été presque complète" (IV, 129). Marcel himself conjectures that Albertine sees in him Andrée, subtly suggesting that he, too, understands the woman's pursuit of the Mother. Moreover, this supposition suggests what many have seen as the narrator's own homosexuality. At one point he distinguishes between those inverted males who reject women entirely and those who find advantages in contact with lesbian women. This second group of men, Morel among them, "jouent pour la femme qui aime les femmes le rôle d'une autre femme, et la femme leur offre en même temps à peu près ce qu'ils trouvent chez l'homme . . ." (III, 24). Furthermore, another mirror scene, in contrast to the moment of recognition when Marcel sees himself, à la Andrée, as part of a same sex couple, implies that he cannot see himself in a heterosexual one. Dining with Saint-Loup and Rachel in a private room, he discovers in the mirror someone "hideux, inconnu" (II, 469).

There is nothing new in the association of lesbianism and motherhood and so initially it might appear simplistic to renew this alliance. Freud felt that the lesbian couple wished to recreate the mother-daughter bond, and in so doing showed the couple's lack of esteem for the father (*Introductory Lectures* 130). And theories since Freud (those of Deutsch, Caprio, Bergler and C. L. Bacon, for example) have continued to emphasize the maternal role. However, all these theories are synonymous with regression while, in dramatic contrast, object relations theory potentially liberates women through the mother-daughter relationship. Imbued with the interpenetration, the lack of separateness, which characterizes the mother-daughter bond, women bring to the female couple qualities the heterosexual bond cannot create. Each woman understands how the (M)other has suffered and how, consequently, she needs to be soothed and protected. Both understand the "I" of the (M)other because they perceive it in themselves, allowing for a beneficial merger of sentience. Each woman accedes to power because the omnipotent and menacing (M)other the male wishes to tame and control is non-threateningly present in both partners.

In short, for most Proustian women the homoerotic, which by virtue of mother-daughter primary love has more primitive weight, supplants the heteroerotic. They take the three components of Dinnerstein's sexual assymetry and stand them on their head, privileging female primacy instead of male. Wanting *direct* access to the Mother these females look to other women. Indeed, this can explain why Albertine ultimately never settles for Marcel no matter how close his resemblance to Andrée, why she implies that lesbianism has a certain cachet (III, 235), and why Marcel is probably right when he interprets the boisterous singing Saint-Loup hears when attempting to bribe Mme Bontemps as pure joy at her new-found freedom. Thus, exclusive male possession turns into an exclusive female world where, no longer under the dominion of male fear, female feelings and sexual impulsivity are set free. In fact, after Albertine's death, Andrée tells the narrator that her friend only remained with him to restrain these needs, hoping he would marry her.

Jane Flax adds, in her discussion of the dual female need for nurturance and autonomy, "Our sense of self is bound up with other women in an intensity and depth simply not present in relations with men" (179). Proustian women may punish the Mother in whose shadow they are trying to establish autonomy but their cruelty is marked by ambivalence because these women can never completely forget the Mother as nurturer, she who put them where they are. Gilberte may be embarrassed by Odette's presence at her parties but her mother is never banished the way Swann, her father, is through name changes and convenient memory loss after his death. What these women want in the female couple is to forgo choosing either nurturance or autonomy as they feel they must with their own mothers and to create an ideal mother-daughter relationship of equality in which the two partners have both. Perhaps this is why Gilberte strikes up a friendship with Andrée at the end of the novel.

When Dinnerstein cites Colette's description of a lesbian couple in *La Vagabonde* ("the melancholy and touching image of two weak creatures who have perhaps sought shelter in each other's arms, there to sleep and weep, safe from man who is so often cruel, and there to taste, better than any pleasure, the bitter happiness of feeling themselves akin, frail and forgotten"), she points out that the women are protecting each other from what men want to do to them *as well as what women want to do to one another*. Indeed, the heterosexual construct requires women's rivalry for men. The homosexual construct allows them to sidestep the renunciation of primary love and to promote solidarity among themselves. Irigaray notes:

> La femme a besoin d'aller découvrir ce qu'elle est, dans des lieux entre femmes, en sortant d'une situation de marchandise et de rivalité où on l'a toujours placée, en redécouvrant son corps par le biais du corps des autres femmes, la tendresse, l'amour, y compris d'ailleurs l'amour maternel. Il y a une fonction de sororité mais aussi de maternage réciproque dans les groupes de femmes. Il y a les horreurs des mères mauvaises, des mères phalliques mais aussi la tendresse de l'entre-maternage. (1981, 61)

Furthermore, many of those familiar with the lesbian relationship, such as a group of feminist writers, theorists and academics brought together in a 1984 conference, describe it as "probably the most intense of all romantic relationships and the most egalitarian" (Boston Lesbian Psychologies Collective 5). This statement is not surprising, most notably because Proust himself points out that everyone sees his or her love object choice as the most satisfying. What does prove interesting is how this group finds object relations theory particularly helpful in understanding this couple and cites works by Chodorow (*The Reproduction of Mothering*), Gilligan (*In a Different Voice*) and Flax ("The Conflict Between Nurturance and Autonomy in Mother-Daughter Relationships and Within Feminism") as offering insights into female development and relationship style that "could be applied explicitly to the lesbian experience" (1). Significantly, many of the observations which emerged from this conference have a counterpart in Proust.

First of all, the novelist lends an explicitness to male homosexuality—even if often under metaphorical cover—that he does not afford his lesbians. Their eroticism is limited to breasts brushing against each other in the Andrée/Albertine waltz (". . . elles sont certainement au comble de la jouissance. On ne sait pas assez que c'est surtout par les seins que les femmes l'éprouvent. Et voyez, les leurs se touchent complètement," notes Cottard [III, 191]); a kiss planted in the neckline of Mlle Vinteuil by her companion ("Dans l'échancrure de son corsage de crêpe Mlle Vinteuil sentit que son amie piquait un baiser . . ." [I, 160]); or perhaps a glib comment by Mme Verdurin to Odette ("Prends garde, je saurai bien te dégeler, tu n'es pas de marbre" [I, 354]). Of course, the author's intimate knowledge of the one and ignorance of the other might explain this difference, but in fact, Nichols points out in "Lesbian Sexuality: Issues and Developing Theory," homosexual men simply are more active (100): they have more frequent sex—Charlus is certainly always at the ready; they have more diverse sexual forms—Jupien's brothel offers as much variety as does any leather bar's back room; and contact with other men does not necessarily threaten what is otherwise seen as a monogamous relationship—Proustian homosexuals are frequently found to make the best husbands. Lesbians prefer closeness and intimacy.

Proust also illustrates a fundamental way lesbians see themselves. Many do not feel that they were born homosexuals but rather that they have elected this identity whereas very few males would characterize themselves as electively homosexual (Golden 32). Indeed, with the exception of Mlle Vinteuil and her companion, no other lesbian-identified woman appears inevitably homosexual. Instead, all of them from Gilberte—whose reddish blonde hair is a symbol of her vacillating nature [Miguet 567]—to Mme Verdurin, fluctuating between heterosexuality and homosexuality, appear to choose the latter when and where they see fit. Inverted males, on the other hand, are controlled and ultimately overwhelmed by their homosexuality. Charlus is progressively incapable of maintaining a public persona of virility and Saint-Loup, once he has confronted his inversion, gives himself up to it. True bisexuality seems to interest Proustian men not at all. Once again, the Mother as first love object explains this dichotomy because it favors a triangulation of the oedipal situation (father added to the mother-daughter dyad) in females that does not occur in males.

Moreover, this triangulation leads to but another explanation of the animosity between mothers and daughters. When a daughter chooses a male love object, she replaces the father but never the mother who, because the male simply joined the female pair, is never displaced in the oedipal situation. However, when the daughter chooses another woman as love object she is substituting someone else for the Mother, saying in effect to the Mother that she loves another woman more than her. The older woman feels rejection (Zitter 178). Thus, it is necessary to add to what only seems the social rejection of Odette and Mme de Villeparisis, for example, a psychological repudiation in the form of their daughters', Gilberte's and Orione's, suspected lesbianism, a phenomenon that Miller overlooks when he talks of the daughter's betrayal.

In many other respects Proust's portrayal of lesbians is valid. For one thing, his numbers are right. To make lesbian women so numerous ("Gomorrhe était dispersée aux quatre coins du monde" [III, 533]) is to reflect statistics: one out of every ten women is a lesbian—although I should point out that this includes women who relate to both sexes (Rohrbaugh 283). Admittedly there are the occasional "femmes hommasses" such as Mme de Vaugoubert or actresses on stage in male clothing such as Odette as Miss Sacripant or women on the street in men's clothing such as Albertine, two types Krafft-Ebing labeled certain lesbians. Yet the author avoids the stereotype of the homosexual woman as bull dyke, she who encompasses all the worst attributes traditionally defined as masculine—tough, aggressive, without emotion and obsessed with sex. In addition, the lifestyle of his lesbians varies: some live with a friend (Mlle Vinteuil), some are married (Oriane and eventually Andrée), while still others have children (Odette and Gilberte).[3]

---

[3] In a bibliography compiled by lesbians, *The Lesbian in Literature,* which rates fictional treatment of the theme, the author of *La Recherche* receives quite good marks. An A indicates major lesbian characters and/or action; B indicates minor lesbian characters and/or action; and C signals latent or repressed lesbianism or characters. An additional rating of T is for trash. A single asterisk shows above average interest; two means substantial quality; and three mean the work is clearly exceptional. Proust covers all the bases: *A la recherche du temps perdu* receives A*, B** and C* while his short story "Avant la nuit" receives an A** rating.

Curiously, it is Colette who, while praising Proust's characterization of male homosexuality, reproaches the novelist for imposing his vision of male reality onto the female universe, portraying Gomorrah with the same powerful sovereignty that men hold in a phallic and patriarchal social order (Stockinger 92):

> there is no such thing as Gomorrah. Puberty, boarding school, solitude, prisons, aberrations, snobbishness—they are all seedbeds, but too shallow to engender and sustain a vice that could attract a great number or become an established thing that would gain the indispensable solidarity of its votaries. Intact, enormous, eternal, Sodom looks down from its heights upon its puny counterfeit. (*The Pure and the Impure*, 131-32)

I strongly disagree. What is powerful about Proust's portrait is not necessarily sociological but psychological. Ironically, Colette, who herself held in high esteem the mother-daughter relationship, fails to see how it supports a female underworld which threatens patriarchy through its potential to eliminate men entirely. Perhaps it is because this is something that, according to Jane Rule, Colette would have found impossible to do (138).

Yet this is why Albertine is so frightening to Marcel. It is not so much that he never arrives at a cohesive narrative which explains her bewildering sexual history or that his mania for control fails to confine the young woman within a discourse of his own making, but rather that Albertine has the means to elude him at will, appearing always precariously balanced between choices that lead her to other women—a matinée at the Trocadéro to see Léa or a visit to Mme Verdurin's to see Mlle Vinteuil. Ultimately it is of little import whether Marcel has any definitive knowledge of her lesbianism or not. What is significant is that femaleness includes its possibility:

> Qu'est-ce que cache le mensonge dans les signes amoureux? Tous les signes mensongers émis par une femme aimée convergent vers un même monde secret: le monde de Gomorrhe, qui, lui non plus, ne dépend pas de telle ou telle femme (quoiqu'une femme puisse l'incarner

> mieux qu'une autre), mais est la possibilité féminine par excellence, comme un *a priori* que la jalousie découvre. C'est que le monde exprimé par la femme aimée est toujours un monde qui nous exclut, même quand elle nous donne une marque de préférence. (Deleuze 16-17)

Thus, Albertine continually holds within her the potential for a world which happily excludes men: "Lesbians, it would seem to the narrator, inhabit a space beyond appropriation by the imagination—they are not specular 'others,' as women are to men, defined in relation to men, but absolutely 'other,' entirely outside the specular sexual economy" (Gray-McDonald 342). When Marcel first sees Albertine, at a period in his life when he thinks that truth lies beyond his immediate experience, he thinks he will make a "doubly glamourous discovery of the life of the sea and the erotic immorality of cruel, sensual girls" (Bersani 37). His expectations are met: it is the life of the *mer/mère* which explains the young girls' sexuality and, furthermore, which makes Albertine, essence of the sea and key to its secret way of life, inevitably emblematic of all women. Marcel understands that he is doomed to separateness, to exclusion, because women's nature makes the sexual symmetry he desires out of the question. That is why Marcel periodically feels the need to be free of Albertine. He understands the futility of his quest and contemplates a new life with other desires.

Consequently, Albertine's death is inevitable—and certainly not dependent on the death of Alfred Agostinelli, Proust's chauffeur whom so many insist on seeing as the sole model for the narrator's mistress. The most prominent foreshadowing is, appropriately, Albertine's threat to jump into the sea, for as Marcel points out, it would imitate Sappho's suicide. Moreover, this merging with the sea is the recovery of the *mer/mère* in the lesbian relationship, which Albertine chooses when she leaves Paris. Indeed, in the 1922 *Albertine disparue,* the young woman, when she does die, dies "au bord de la Vivonne." Marcel reads Vivonne in the telegram but sees Montjouvain and understands that his mistress has left him to join Mlle Vinteuil and her friend, neatly entwining motherhood (water imagery) and lesbianism. Textually, a passage describing the Vivonne as what gives the Guermantes Way its charm directly precedes the notorious Montjouvain scene and Montjouvain, "située au bord d'une grande mare," (I, 145) is itself associated with water. Furthermore the crucial positioning of the lesbian theme—unequivocally announced as it is well in advance of the male homosexuality motif—underscores its importance as a major textual thread. Its more intimate connection to motherhood, reciprocal love which excludes men, establishes the primacy of lesbianism and makes male inversion its offshoot.

Indeed, remarkably noteworthy are the numerous lesbians associated with water or, even more significant, those whose activities take place near water and who, thus, continue this equation established in Combray. (Men whose inversion appears directly accountable to the Mother find themselves by the water as well—Charlus, Saint-Loup and the young Cambremer.) In addition to Albertine, Andrée is synonymous with the Normandy beach resort, but while in Balbec the narrator also discovers the lesbian actress Léa, Bloch's cousin Esther Lévy who lives with her, and Bloch's sister who scandalizes the Grand Hôtel clientele by her public behavior with a former actress. Moreover, other places known for their water, of one sort or another, underscore the supposed lesbianism of additional female characters. Odette is linked to Bade and Nice where "elle avait eu une sorte de notoriété galante" (I, 307). The Baronne de Putbus's chambermaid, reputedly bisexual, was to accompany her mistress "d'abord aux eaux en Allemagne, puis à Biarritz, et pour finir, chez Mme Verdurin" (III, 150). Appropriately, Mme Verdurin's residence at that moment was La Raspelière, the Normandy beach home rented from the Cambremers.

The principal lesbian figure, Albertine, does not limit herself to Balbec but is also associated with women in such other cities as Cherbourg and Amsterdam, the latter provoking the narrator to say: "Cet amour entre femmes était quelque chose de trop inconnu, dont rien ne permettait d'imaginer avec certitude, avec justesse, les plaisirs, la qualité" (III, 887). Trying to ply information from his mistress, Marcel suggested that he already knew a great deal, as the narrator had done while questioning Albertine about a woman she had known in Vichy. The Vichy reference seems to bring full circle her group of lesbian friends because it resonates with an earlier conversation between the two in which Albertine explains how, while in Montjouvain with Mlle Vinteuil and her companion, they tried a variety of "eau gazeuse," notably "l'eau de Vichy."

Added to all this is Albertine's apparent preference for women whose work brings them in contact with water. She had a flirtation with a "doucheuse" and Morel, who met Albertine at Mme Verdurin's, would find "pêcheuses" and "blanchisseuses," form them to his own taste, and then turn them over to the young woman. The narrator even goes so far as to use marine imagery to describe the eye contact he thought his companion was making with another woman: "On eût dit qu'elle lui faisait des signes comme à l'aide d'un phare" (III, 245). Finally, Marcel makes clear all women's potential lesbianism when he comments, "La conversation d'une femme qu'on aime ressemble à un sol qui recouvre une eau souterraine et dangereuse . . ." (III, 406).

Interestingly enough, Mlle de Stermaria, who serves as a prelude to the narrator's mother/mistress reconciliation efforts and whom Marcel discovers before Albertine, seems to encompass this possibility herself. She is connected to both Albertine and Mlle Vinteuil through Marcel's initial focus on her cheeks compared to the Vivonne water lilies. But, more important, this oblique water reference is expanded in the very meaning of her name. Brichot, in one of his impromptu etymology lectures, explains that *Ster* in Breton means water. Thus, it is doubly fitting that when the narrator returns to Paris and makes arrangements to dine with the Breton woman, curiously and inexplicably divorced after only three months of marriage, he expressly chooses an island in the Bois. However, when Mme de Stermaria backs out of the engagement, she leaves the impression that it is specifically in this water bound region that she is unwilling to see him.

Even more significant is the name of the island where the couple planned to dine, *L'île des Cygnes,* for the homophony with *signes* brings to mind that lesbianism is the one sign that remains indecipherable for men. This island resonates with Odette's experience with a neighboring female diner who invited her to disappear "derrière le petit rocher voir l'effet du clair de lune sur l'eau" (I, 359). In fact this island unleashes a network of associations. The word *cygne,* or swan, recalls the scene between Albertine and a laundress in which the narrator's companion offers her foot to be kissed. When Aimé describes the encounter, the result of an investigation Marcel asked him to do after Albertine's death, the narrator thinks of two Elstir paintings. In one, a young girl imitates Albertine's gesture and with the other foot pushes her friend into the water. The second girl resists and her raised thigh reminds Marcel of a swan's neck, "le même méandre de cou de cygne avec l'angle du genou, que faisait la chute de la cuisse d'Albertine quand elle était à côté de moi sur le lit . . ." (IV, 108). Marcel places next to this woman as swan Leda and contemplates the "double nudité de marbres féminins," a description which echoes Mme Verdurin's words to Odette that she could titillate her because she was not, after all, made of marble. Furthermore, Leda is too close to Léa not to recall the lesbian actress.

Ultimately the narrator must accept the evidence that he has loved a woman who was not his "genre" because she was "mauvais genre." By the time Marcel travels to Venice with his mother, a trip planned many years before when he believed reciprocal love beyond the Mother possible, he knows it is not possible. His last ditch attempt to pursue a woman—when he sees "Baronne Putbus et suite" in the hotel register and wants to remain for the "plaisirs charnels" her maid might offer—is thwarted by the Mother herself. She refuses to delay the return home, and simultaneously the Venetian waters become forbidding: ". . . ce bassin de l'Arsenal à la fois insignifiant et lointain me remplissait de ce mélange de dégoût et d'effroi que j'avais éprouvé tout enfant la première fois que j'accompagnai ma mère aux bains Deligny. . ." (IV, 232). Thus, in truth, Albertine's death marks the discovery that sexual symmetry—reunion with the Mother—exists in a world for women only. The novel becomes a therapeutic exercise which compels the narrator not only to confront his feelings about females but, however subtly, to examine his own sexuality as well. The telling of Albertine's story becomes the rewriting of his own: "Ce n'était pas Albertine seule qui n'était qu'une succession de moments, c'était aussi moi-même" (IV, 71).

Chapter Five

"Mommy Dearest"

Because the ideal union Marcel seeks emerges as only possible between women, the grandmother and mother assume a new position amid the Proustian patterns: they are the *sine qua non* of a relationship the narrator will never know, and Proust's portraits of women reflect the narrator's disillusionment. What ultimately takes place is the unflattering transformation of women Marcel initially admired, Oriane de Guermantes for example, as well as the increasing prominence of those, such as Rachel, he had always held in contempt. Most important, the grandmother and mother drop from view and motherhood is demystified, disdained and, in short, dethroned from its position of ideal feminine role.

A curious early anecdote captures this fundamental, dare I say, sea change in *La Recherche:* while on an evening ride with a friend of his father, the narrator is captivated by an unknown woman passing by. He jumps out of the carriage to follow her, and when, after a breathless run through the streets of Paris, he finally comes upon the "inconnue" under a streetlight, he finds himself face to face with Mme Verdurin (II, 73). Similarly, throughout the novel Marcel pursues an "inconnue," the woman whose sexuality unflaggingly sustains her as the unknown. Increasingly disillusioned, he provides degenerating portraits of the feminine until he ultimately confronts she who is responsible for this deception. Moreover, leaving his father's friend behind, the narrator signals his inability to identify with the paternal. This choice diminishes his chances at heterosexuality, an opportunity already foreclosed by his discovery of the Mother's role in sexual relations.

Thus, Mme Verdurin becomes the author's most reprehensible portrait, and by the novel's close, because she has co-opted all its women—even the mother and grandmother—in importance, she remains alone as a Proustian example of the feminine, more particularly, the Mother fallen from grace. And not unintentionally, Proust introduces La Patronne directly following Combray. By placing her immediately after Tante Léonie, he presents side by side the two most successful women among those who wish to reign in their respective worlds. In telescoped form is a relationship which lends a particular structure to the novel: not only does the narrator's aunt prefigure Mme Verdurin, eventual queen of the Faubourg Saint-Germain, but their similarity gives symmetry to the gallery of females which intervenes.

Indeed, each volume of *La Recherche* has a woman at its center. However, these women reach their central role through a type of relay race in which two women seem momentarily to compete for prominence, one finally relents, and she prepares the way for the second's dominance. This pattern is repeated until Mme Verdurin who began the race finally wins. In *Du côté de chez Swann,* Mme Verdurin and Odette alternately enjoy textual importance which Odette assumes entirely in "Nom de pays: le nom" ("Autour de Mme Swann"). There she shares her premier role with Gilberte, whose portrait prepares Albertine's. Odette initially has center stage in *A l'ombre des jeunes filles en fleurs* then bows to Albertine. Oriane, naturally the significant woman in *Le Côté de Guermantes* is, nonetheless, eclipsed midway by Albertine before she recoups her dominance. Albertine takes over in *Sodome et Gomorrhe, La Prisonnière* and *La Fugitive* until Mme Verdurin vanquishes everyone in *Le Temps retrouvé*. The development of these women's significance reduced to—Mme Verdurin/Odette/Gilberte(Albertine)/Odette/Albertine/Oriane/Albertine/MmeVerdurin reveals both Albertine and Mme Verdurin as key to the novel's structure—the first for her longevity and the second for the bookend effect she creates.

Whereas Tante Léonie's bed is her theatre, Mme Verdurin's is the "petit noyau," and she is a superb actress whose "fidèles" are an appreciative audience. However, in contrast to the other female performers of *La Recherche,* La Patronne has learned to limit her acting to pantomime and has a repertoire of symbolic gestures, making her performance a caricature also. Since the accident to her jaw, Mme Verdurin, rather than truly laughing, gives the sign of laughter, covering her face and pretending to stifle overwhelming guffaws. Mme Verdurin, like Tante Léonie who enjoyed exacerbating the Françoise-Eulalie rivalry, has her favorite *mises en scène*. In a good cop-bad cop scenario her husband publicly harrasses the timid Saniette for not enunciating clearly: " 'Pauvre Saniette, je ne veux pas que vous le rendiez malheureux', dit Mme Verdurin sur un ton de fausse pitié et pour ne laisser un doute à personne sur l'intention insolente de son mari" (III, 325). But La Patronne is also quite capable of a one woman show, and after M. Verdurin's death, she singlehandedly diminishes Brichot in front of her guests by reading his newspaper articles aloud, pointing out their inanities.

True to Proust's system, Mme Verdurin's superiority as an actress goes hand in hand with an insensitivity which moves her unhesitatingly through the social ranks. Death is meaningless to La Patronne, aids and abets her climb to the top, and in fact, by the time she arrives in the Faubourg Saint-Germain, she is standing on a stack of cadavers. Her husband had served her well during his lifetime ("Il n'avait jamais d'avis qu'après sa femme, dont son rôle particulier était de mettre à exécution les désirs, ainsi que les désirs des fidèles, avec de grandes ressources d'ingéniosité" [I, 188]), but rather than being saddened by his death, Mme Verdurin simply seeks an efficacious replacement. The widowed and financially ruined Duc de Duras serves as a useful transition. (Appropriately, in Combray "les dames de la rue de l'Oiseau . . . avaient dit en ricanant 'la duchesse de Duras', comme si c'eût été un rôle que Mme Verdurin eût tenu au théâtre" [IV, 533].) After his death, La Patronne unabashedly moves on to her third and most important partner, the Prince de Guermantes who, impoverished by the German defeat, is only too willing to make the wealthy woman his wife. However, the most useful death is Vinteuil's, for the foundation of La Patronne's success is the deceased composer's music. Her salon passes for a "Temple de la musique" where, people say, Vinteuil found his inspiration, justifying Mme Verdurin's view of herself as a patron of the arts.

Most significant, Mme Verdurin is a "mère méchante," for the "petit noyau" is not simply a salon orchestrated by La Patronne but, also, a family guided by the Mère Verdurin. Initially, everything in her salon is *en famille*. Her family members know she and her husband need not invite them to dinner because "on avait chez eux 'son couvert mis' " (I, 186). They need not wear dinner clothes nor is there a set program that demands that someone entertain. This intimate atmosphere allows her children to shine, and Mme Verdurin is an excessively adoring mother. She finds Cottard to have "plus de diagnostic que Potain" and, to her mind, Dechambre " 'enfonçait' à la fois Planté et Rubenstein" (I, 185). At La Raspelière, she explains to Mme de Cambremer: "Ce n'est pas de la musiquette qu'on fait ici. En art vous savez, les fidèles de mes mercredis, mes enfants comme je les appelle, c'est effrayant ce qu'ils sont avancés . . ." (III, 319-20).

Mme Verdurin employs a variety of techniques to ensure her chidren's fidelity. One of her favorites is the maternal ploy of reward for good behavior, promising those who "ne lâchent pas" that their get-together will be even better the next time. Like the stereotypical mother she also uses food to exact the behavior she wishes. All her gatherings are built around a meal and to attract the narrator and Albertine to La Raspelière, she notes the poor quality of cuisine everywhere else, saying of the highly touted galette at Rivebelle: ". . . on ne sait pas avec quoi c'est fait. Je connais une pauvre fille à qui cela a donné une péritonite qui l'a enlevée en trois jours" (III, 360). Possessiveness, however, is Mme Verdurin's most noteworthy negative maternal characteristic and pushes her to be jealous of her clan members' real families: ". . . elle . . . haïssait les familles (ce dissolvant du petit noyau) . . . elle me dit: 'C'est du reste si ennuyeux les familles, on n'aspire qu'à en sortir' . . ." (III, 301). She is particularly jealous of other mothers who might jeopardize her role. When Dechambre's aunt demands that he dine at his mother's New Year's Day, Mme Verdurin ridicules this habit as exceedingly provincial.

In short, the Mère Verdurin is a tyrannical mother who demands the same adoration the narrator's mother gives so naturally to the grandmother. (*Mère* is always used pejoratively as a title. Oriane comments: "Tenez, regardez la mère Rampillon, trouvez-vous une grande différence entre ça et un squelette en robe ouverte?" [III, 84].) However, whereas Proust appeared close to canonizing the grandmother, he gives us a satire of sainthood in the portrait of Mme Verdurin, travesty of the Holy Mother. And he suggests the ultimate conflation of the two portraits—the movement from adoration of the Mother to aversion—in a description of the Virgin Mary in Balbec's church: ". . . c'était elle enfin, l'œuvre d'art immortelle et si longtemps désirée, que je trouvais métamorphosée, ainsi que l'église elle-même, en une petite vieille de pierre dont je pouvais mesurer la hauteur et compter les rides" (II, 21). Mme Verdurin, comparable to her Combray counterpart seen at one moment as "la Vierge défaillante" and who welcomed supplicants by her nightstand, a "maître-autel," receives worshippers in her "petite église," whose orthodoxy the faithful were never to question. Seated on a chair which looms above all others, La Patronne seems on a pedestal surrounded by her followers as well as by a multitude of gifts placed at her shrine by the faithful. And appropriately enough, Cottard attends Mme Verdurin's receptions during the war in a military uniform decorated with a ribbon reminiscent of "celui des 'Enfants de Marie' " (IV, 349). Nonetheless, Mme Verdurin is anxious on holy days should some other religion distract her "fidèles," and she becomes ill at the very thought of Christmas or Holy Week, explaining:

> qu'elle était le seul général à qui dût obéir sa légion, comme le Christ ou le Kaiser, que celui qui aimait son père et sa mère autant qu'elle et n'était pas prêt à les quitter pour la suivre n'était pas digne d'elle, qu'au lieu de s'affaiblir au lit ou de se laisser berner par une grue, ils feraient mieux de rester près d'elle, elle, seul remède et seule volupté. (III, 270)

Thus, when all is said and done, Mme Verdurin is a caricature whose hyperbolic contours circumscribe Marcel's worst fear, a female authority whose negative qualities have their impact where they can do the most harm and whose power can render men helpless. She is the "dangerous and cold" woman described by men who have had "too much mother" (Chodorow 85).

There is a second prominent example of aberrant motherhood—Charlus. First of all, like Mme Verdurin, he is the member of a decidedly unconventional clan, the Guermantes. With the exception of Mme de Marsantes there are no biological mothers: The mother/daughter relationship is replaced by the aunt/niece duo which, Oriane and Mme de Villeparisis (who, herself, was raised by an aunt) illustrate, bears witness to the interpenetration of *surrogate* mother and child. Oriane and her aunt share the same niggardliness which extends from money matters to human matters even though they project a veneer of social grace which they dramatize with "bonne campagnarde" simplicity. Both are known for an appreciation of art—each paints watercolors—and "esprit." Finally, Mme de Villeparisis and the Duchesse de Guermantes share the same philosophy—"seuls l'intelligence, le cœur, le talent ont de l'importance" (II,

741)—none of which does either have, although Mme de Villeparisis's *Mémoires* should not go unnoticed. Furthermore, the aunt/niece alliance favors the same social leverage as does the mother-daughter relationship. Consequently, Mme de Villeparisis, who had chosen to pursue her liberalism to the limit and found herself an outcast in the *haut monde,* hand picks her niece's husband and assures social prestige for Oriane as well as herself.

Because the Guermantes seem to revert to a medieval tradition which places paternity in the uncle's hands, fatherless Saint-Loup is in large part under the guidance of Charlus. Thus, the *"tante"*/*neveu* relationship is as important as that of *tante*/*nièce* in this family. Speaking of Maréchal d'Huxelles's wife, Charlus uses this slang term for a homosexual male himself: "On pourrait faire d'après elle la synthèse lyrique de la 'Femme d'une Tante'. D'abord hommasse; généralement la femme d'une Tante est un homme, c'est ce qui lui rend si facile de lui faire des enfants" (III, 808). And just as with the female couple, there is the same confusion between Robert and his Oncle Palamède. Homosexual, Saint-Loup, "en vrai neveu de M. de Charlus" (IV, 256), acts out the farce of many mistresses. He uses the very same techniques. When the narrator sees Saint-Loup swaddled in the skirts of his supposed lover, he sees "une sorte de répétition involontaire d'un geste ancestral que j'avais pu observer chez M. de Charlus, comme enrobé dans les atours de Mme Molé ou d'une autre, bannière d'une cause *gynophile* qui n'était pas la sienne . . ." (IV, 263). Indeed, Marcel describes him as the successor in a role once played by Charlus, and ultimately their love for Morel seals their similarity.

Nonetheless, the baron surpasses his nephew and it is his very femaleness which makes him so singular: ". . . ce corps qui avait bien compris ce que M. de Charlus avait cessé d'entendre, déploya, au point que le baron eût mérité l'épithète de *lady-like,* toutes les séductions d'une grande dame" (III, 300). Not only is his the characterization of a woman trapped inside a man, but the baron also encompasses the novelist's dual definition of femininity. On the one hand, his extraordinary acting talents, enhanced by his voice and physical presence, allow him to surpass all other women in theatricality. And as one of high society's most powerful members, he could choose his daily *mise en scène,* inventing a duel, for example, to bring back Morel: "Je crois que ce sera bien beau . . . Voir Sarah Bernhardt dans *L'Aiglon,* qu'est-ce que c'est? du caca. Mounet-Sully dans *Œdipe?*

caca . . . qu'est-ce que c'est à côté de cette chose inouïe, voir batailler le propre descendant du Connétable?" (III, 456-57). In short, he provides what Sedgwick calls an "endlessly lavish production" of the spectacle of the closet (223).

Charlus's multiple metamorphoses also place him with Proustian women. But the baron's physical changes, in contrast to Odette's, for example, do not move him up the social ladder but follow his fall. They parallel the growing dominance of his homosexuality, and most important, they transform Charlus from a comic character into a tragic figure. Proust's technique of bringing characters in and out of the shadows heightens reader reaction, and each time the baron appears, the transformation is startling. Yet, there is always a hint of what will follow so that the novelist builds the baron's dotage and pederasty in the same way he slowly prepares Albertine's lesbianism. When Marcel sees Charlus in Balbec, his sartorial fastidiousness and wild look—eyes which dart everywhere—are the subtle suggestion of his sexual proclivities and subsequent mental imbalance. Certain scenes are particularly memorable in Proust's catalogue of the baron's downfall: Charlus crossing the Guermantes courtyard, softened and womanly in his solitude; or an aged baron crossing the waiting room in the Doncières train station, an actor out of costume but still wearing his make-up. By the novel's end "un enfant, sans la fierté qu'ils ont, c'était ce qu'il était devenu . . ." (IV, 439).

Furthermore, Charlus takes the personality traits he shares with Proustian women to incomparable lengths. He surpasses Mme Bontemps in anti-semitism, Rachel in revenge and Oriane in snobbishness. The baron's wrath is all the more venomous because it is seemingly unfounded. His rage against Mme de Sainte-Euverte is incomprehensible and even less understandable is his hatred of the Comtesse Molé whom he once adored. His ill will does not exclude his family, and he writes an angry and insolent letter to Mme de Villeparisis threatening to expose her parsimony—she had reimbursed Charlus money borrowed from him but minus the cost of wiring it. In short, no one could possibly equal his verbal abuse, for "chez M. de Charlus les louanges immodérées étaient clamées avec un véritable éclat d'éloquence, et assaisonnées des plus fines, des plus mordantes railleries . . ." (III, 43).

On the other hand, seemingly refusing subsumption under a coherent interpretive system (Sedgwick 226), Charlus has some remarkably good qualities which would ostensibly align him with the narrator's mother and grandmother. Indeed, he has the latter's warmest approbation, as does, interestingly enough, Robert de Saint-Loup. Marcel's grandmother admires the baron's sensitivity which, though it prompts certain stereotypical homosexual preoccupations such as home furnishings and women's clothing (his nickname is the "Couturière" [III, 713]), also produces artistic talent. The narrator describes him as a "pianiste délicieux, un peintre amateur qui n'était pas sans goût, un éloquent discoureur" (III, 344). In addition, Charlus possesses a goodness which threads the refrain "bon cœur" throughout the baron's portrait. Even Morel remembers Charlus as "[un] homme ayant le plus d'idées élevées qu'il eût jamais connu, un homme d'une sensibilité extraordinaire, une manière de saint" (IV, 346).

However, it is Charlus's comprehension of Mme de Sévigné which best demonstrates his supposed difference from Proustian women and which most inspires the grandmother's admiration. During the same conversation when Mme de Villeparisis showed her inability to understand the relationship between the seventeenth-century writer and her daughter, the baron remarks instead: "C'est si beau ce qu'elle dit quand elle la quitte: 'Cette séparation me fait une douleur à l'âme, que je sens comme un mal du corps'" (II, 121). Extraordinarily pleased to hear someone speak of her model as she herself would have and astonished that it is a man, the grandmother finds Charlus to have feminine sensibilities. She is even more impressed when the baron stresses to his aunt the importance of simply being with those one loves, and that furthermore, "l'important dans la vie n'est pas ce qu'on aime . . . c'est d'aimer . . . Les démarcations trop étroites que nous traçons autour de l'amour viennent seulement de notre grande ignorance de la vie" (II, 122).

Apparently the key to Charlus's systematic character contradictions and their unparalleled extremes is his homosexuality. Influenced by contemporary thought, Proust is simply expressing an assumption of his day (Rivers 14). Charlus is a woman within a man, and the novelist equates this paradox with the baron's erratic behavior. After witnessing the sexual encounter between the baron and Jupien, Marcel observes:

> la transmutation de M. de Charlus en une personne nouvelle était si complète que non seulement les contrastes de son visage, de sa voix, mais rétrospectivement les hauts et les bas eux-mêmes de ses relations

> avec moi, tout ce qui avait paru jusque-là incohérent à mon esprit, devenait intelligible, se montrait évident . . . De plus je comprenais maintenant pourquoi tout à l'heure, quand je l'avais vu sortir de chez Mme de Villeparisis, j'avais pu trouver que M. de Charlus avait l'air d'une femme: c'en était une! (III, 16)

Charlus owes his femininity to the Mother. Not only is the baron's adoration of his dead mother singular, far exceeding Basin's devotion, but also the maternal influence is so great that Charlus is a visual tribute to his mother's memory. He is an excellent example (as is Saint-Loup) of what Proust calls "les mères profanées" (III, 300), a theme as inexhaustible and difficult as the baron's own homosexuality and to which it is inextricably linked (Sedgwick 223). "Il a toujours été le portrait de ma belle-mère; mais c'est encore plus frappant maintenant" (IV, 570), observes Oriane. Although the narrator points out that this theme is worthy of further reflexion ("Mais laissons ici ce qui mériterait un chapître à part. . ."), he never formally develops it. Two of the Pléiade editors, Antoine Campagnon and Pierre Edmond Robert, note that this leitmotif, found in both "La Confession d'une jeune fille" and the Montjouvain scene, is mentioned in Carnet I (1908)—"Le visage maternel dans un petit fils débauché"—and repeated in 1909 drafts: "Le visage d'un fils qui vit, ostensoir où mettait toute sa foi une sublime mère morte, est comme une profanation de ce souvenir sacré" (III, 1514). To my mind, because the profaned mother and inversion, whether male or female, are intimately tied, all of *La Recherche* becomes their elaboration, with uncloseted Charlus as its most egregious example.

Thus, the novelist's choice of a nickname for Palamède is thoroughly appropriate. Mémé, also the familiar term for grandmother, labels the baron with the maternal role he will eventually play. Ironically, when Charlus meets the narrator and Brichot on his way to Mme Verdurin's and says, "Je vous ai dérangés, vous aviez l'air de vous amuser comme deux petites folles, et vous n'aviez pas besoin d'une vieille grand-maman rabat-joie comme moi" (III, 715), he suggests a second familiar expression. And *mémère*—"grosse femme d'un certain âge"—is what he progressively becomes: ". . . une vieille femme maniérée comme était M. de Charlus . . . trahit de plus en plus d'efféminement, dans ses risibles affectations de virilité . . ." (III, 847). Indeed, Charlus's desire to succeed at motherhood ("j'étais né pour être bonne d'enfant" [III, 798]) dominates his homosexuality and is the theme which unifies his important relationships. Proust is in fact quite specific about this tendency in certain gay males. In a textual variation entitled "La Race des Tantes," he speaks of homosexuals as "quelques uns [sic] maternels épris de dévouement, cherchant toute leur vie à faire . . . un député ou à trouver du travail pour un maçon . . . " (III, 927). These liaisons leave the impression that the baron wants to rear not ravish his protégés ("Pour les jeunes gens . . . je ne désire aucune possession physique . . ." [III, 13]), and he explains to the narrator that there is nothing more satisfying than to expend one's efforts in the education and formation of a worthy individual.

Of course, the relationship which best illustrates Charlus's wish to mother is Morel, and in fact, when Charlus was overcome with a "maniaque envie d'adopter" people feared he had Charlie in mind. The baron behaves like a proud parent, admiring everything about the young man from his cardplaying to the way his hair falls—"La Mèche!"—when he plays the violin. He advances his success whenever and however he can, asking the narrator to speak to Bergotte about a possible writing career for Morel: "Je sais bien que je m'exagère facilement quand il s'agit de lui, comme toutes les vieilles mamans gâteaux du Conservatoire" (III, 726). Later, Morel does write and uses his work, "Les Mésaventures d'une douairière en us, les vieux jours de la baronne" (IV, 346) for example, to attack Charlus, behavior strikingly reminiscent of that exhibited by Proustian daughters toward their mothers. But the baron's ultimate means of mothering is to arrange Morel's marriage with Jupien's niece, hoping to immobilize the young man by replacing his mysterious desires with those chosen by Charlus himself (Buisine 71). When this plan fails, he adopts the young woman and marries the newly named Mlle d'Oloron—whom Basin intimates is Charlus's illegitimate daughter—to M. and Mme de Cambremer's son. Because he is a homosexual this marriage illustrates to what degree "mothers" discourage any veritable union and promote separation of the sexes in Proust's world.

Ultimately though, the confrontation between Charlus and Mme Verdurin best demonstrates the nefarious role mothers play in Proust's world because the baron is clearly further feminized under her influence. Just the baron's foray into the foreign milieu that is Mme Verdurin's salon exacerbates his femininty: he exhibits his most gracious manners for these *petits bourgeois,* and "On aurait cru voir s'avancer Mme de Marsantes . . ."

(III, 300). More important, Mme Verdurin encourages the Charlus/Morel relationship saying, when the two spend the night at La Raspelière, that if they wish "to make music" they should not hesitate because the walls are thick and no one else is on their floor. Interestingly, this behavior contrasts dramatically with her attitude toward relationships the heterosexual men in her "petit noyau" pursue. La Mère Verdurin intervenes in Brichot's private life and Elstir is no longer a "fidèle" because he chose another woman over La Patronne. Not accidentally, this has a parallel in Proust's life. On the one hand, while Jeanne Proust broke up her son's early love for Marie de Benardaky, on the other hand, she was only too willing to solicit a male's attention for her son, as she did with the Count de Salignac-Fénelon after noticing Marcel's distress at his absence (Hayman 64). Both "mothers" seem determined to prevent reaccess to the Mother in an extrafamilial anaclitic love object and to oblige their "sons" to remain with them.

Thus, Mme Verdurin does not simply push the baron toward further effeminacy, she castrates him. La Mère Verdurin is the phallic mother. Swann's dream at the end of "Un Amour de Swann" illustrates this when the dilettante looks at La Patronne who "le fixa d'un regard étonné durant un long moment pendant lequel il vit sa figure se déformer, son nez s'allonger et qu'elle avait de grandes moustaches" (I, 372). As Bellemin-Noël points out in his analysis of this dream, Mme Verdurin suddenly becomes the phallic mother, viewed as such because Swann sees himself as castrated (53). And a second dream, this time tellingly the narrator's, demonstrates the ambivalence a child feels toward the phallic mother who either accords or refuses the child a phallus. Charlus acts out these feelings against Mme Verdurin, sentiments he had already expressed in his desire to see Bloch "frapper à coups redoublés sur sa charogne . . . de mère" (II, 584):

> j'avais rêvé que M. de Charlus avait cent dix ans et venait de donner une paire de claques à sa propre mère, Mme Verdurin, parce qu'elle avait acheté cinq milliards un bouquet de violettes. . . . (III, 375)

That the phallic mother is equivalent to the preoedipal mother is of no little consequence here. The latter resembles the first not so much because of the mother's perceived physiology but rather because of her power (Chodorow 122). Mme Verdurin is the mighty preoedipal mother in her most menacing form, emphasizing her strength by metamorphosing into a male. Proust's last portrait of La Patronne equips her with a manly voice and a monocle, an ocular accessory otherwise restricted to men. This remarkable transformation expressly parallels the Mère Verdurin's reign as queen of the Faubourg Saint-Germain (which, by the way, the narrator anthropomorphizes as a "douairière gâteuse" [IV, 535]), for it has more than just social significance. Because this success underscores the preoedipal mother's influence in adult sexual arrangements, her triumph has sexual importance as well. Not only is Mme Verdurin's prominence a reminder that the child's preoedipal period is gendered, but it is she whom the adult seeks in a love object. And Mme Verdurin's investment in sexual matters is unmistakable as Swann's dream makes clear. Highlighting her phallic/preoedipal role, the dream also illustrates where it leads: Mme Verdurin facilitates Odette's flight with her lover, but because the "rêve de Swann" couples the two women as well, it signals the Mother's part in homosexuality—female and male alike. The Mother, and not the Father of the celebrated Oedipus Complex, manipulates and decides sexuality.

Indeed, on the one hand, Mme Verdurin, accomplice, serves as *entremetteuse,* or "trait d'union" says Odette admiringly, as she did in the younger woman's relationships with both Swann and Forcheville. Mme Verdurin explains how she counseled Odette with regard to the first man: "Comme elle n'a plus personne en ce moment, je lui ai dit qu'elle devrait coucher avec lui" (I, 224). Once his society connections have placed him in disfavor and La Patronne has chosen M. de Forcheville as Odette's partner, she comments to her husband, "As-tu vu les façons que Swann se permet maintenant avec nous? . . . Alors, qu'il dise tout de suite que nous tenons une maison de rendez-vous!" (I, 280-81). And Swann, in his fury, does not hesitate to label Mme Verdurin "maquerelle, entremetteuse" (I, 282). Furthermore, she does not limit her services to Odette, and her salon contains other signs which seem to say it is a *maison de passe.* Appropriately named La Patronne, she offers rooms at La Raspelière to the narrator and Albertine but eventually tries to promote a relationship between the same young woman and her nephew Octave. In addition, some who frequent the "petit noyau" seem to have exchanged one bordello for another. Mme de Putbus and her *femme de chambre* fall into this category. The first syllable of the baroness's name is an obvious equivalent of *putain:* the "us," "le suffixe du sexe," is suitable for a woman of pleasure, and "bus" calls to mind ". . . (l'omni) bus', ce transport en commun, ou chacun peut 'monter' " (Roger 50). The second woman, Saint-Loup tells the narrator, gives freely of her favors to men and women alike. Because Marcel first mistook her for a madam the Princesse Sherbatoff qualifies as a woman of doubtful reputation. And while Mme Verdurin accuses those women unwilling to greet her in her own home the evening of Charlus's musical extravaganza of being "de vieilles grues," she willingly welcomes the renowned actress and former prostitute Rachel into her salon at the novel's close.

Yet Proust goes even further. He does not simply compare the Verdurin salon to a house of pleasure, an all the more pronounced conflation when Marcel gives furnishings from Tante Léonie, Mme Verdurin's Combray counterpart, to a brothel. But rather, with La Patronne as the Princesse de Guermantes, not only does the novelist collapse all the salons into one, but he also underscores the complete convergence of salon and *maison de passe*. Rachel's presence points up her resemblance to *haut monde* women and corroborates the narrator's earlier statement about the world of prostitution: ". . . les femmes changent si vite de situation dans ce monde-là, quand elles en changent . . ." (II, 456). But many similarities exist, the most obvious of which is the hostess's need—whether Odette, Mme Verdurin or Oriane—to be surrounded by men. Moreover, "On feignait d'ignorer que le corps d'une maîtresse de maison était manié par qui voulait, pourvu que le 'salon' fût demeuré intact" (II, 716). Also a good hostess knows how to encourage fortuitous encounters: when Mme de Villeparisis sees the narrator and the Duchesse de Guermantes in conversation, she does not wish to disturb them: "car les bons offices de l'entremetteuse font partie des devoirs d'une maîtresse de maison" (II, 669). Confusion occurs in the opposite direction also. Swann, in a *maison de rendez-vous*, finds himself talking to a young woman as he might have spoken to Oriane: "Swann ne pouvait s'empêcher de dire à ces filles les mêmes choses qui auraient plu à la princesse des Laumes . . . 'C'est gentil, tu as mis des yeux bleus de la couleur de ta ceinture' " (I, 367). There, of course, is also Mlle de l'Orgeville who privileges the confusion herself, for according to Saint-Loup, the young society woman frequented houses of prostitution.

Because of the coexistence of tawdriness and refinement, *apaches* and *mondains*, the convergence of salon and bordello reaches its zenith in Jupien's brothel. The Prince de Foix and the Vicomte de Courvoisier frequent this house of ill repute as does the Député de l'Action Libérale. Jupien addresses his clients by their first name—the deputy is Monsieur Eugène—bringing to mind high society's snobbish use of nicknames (Grigri, Mémé, Mama, etc.) to publicize one's familiarity with its members. Charlus's role is that of grande dame, making him a mirror image of Mme Verdurin. She turns what is ostensibly a salon into a bordello and he transforms what is really a bordello into a salon.

Le Palace, a *maison de passe* near Balbec, adds sexual confusion to social confusion. At first a meeting place for heterosexuals, it later caters more and more frequently to homosexuals. Confirming his inversion, the Prince de Guermantes has an encounter with Morel there, and appropriately enough since her sexual significance is already evident, one of her guests links Mme Verdurin to Le Palace. (This same guest thinks that Mme Cottard would be right at home as well, and ironically, one of the prostitutes is named Mlle Noémie, a typing correction from Mlle Léontine [III, 1600, n. a]—Mme Cottard's first name.) Contemplating staying there rather than at La Raspelière, he says: ". . . je ne comprends pas pourquoi . . . Mme Verdurin n'est pas venue habiter ici . . . Mme Verdurin y eût joué parfaitement son rôle de patronne" (III, 462). Associated with both the prince and La Patronne this particular brothel prefigures their marriage, definitive sign of Sodom and Gomorrah's union. Indeed, located in Maineville which, the narrator explains, means *media villa,* Le Palace seems the perfect place for those two mutually exclusive groups to meet one another halfway. Proust's explanation is even more revealing when it becomes clear that it appears nowhere in the etymology references he consulted and only shows up on a list of more or less imaginary meanings in Cahier 72 (III, 1600, n. 2).

Ultimately, most significant in this sexual segregation is the (preoedipal) Mother's role: She is responsible for both her son's homosexuality and her daughter's lesbianism. Thus, Proust progressively provides a scathing indictment of the matriarchal domain that is the salon, one which replicates the narrator's movement, beginning in the Swann home, "vers ses flots versatiles. Ce n'était pas encore la grande mer, c'était déjà la lagune" (I, 561). Moreover, he eventually adds a third dimension to his characterization by comparing this sphere to a public restroom. Overcome by nausea, his grandmother asks him to follow her to a Champs-Elysées facility he had been to earlier with Françoise, who'd said that the custodian was actually a marquise belonging to the Saint-Ferréol family. There is even a seeming reference to the homosexual theme which emerges prominently later, a forecast of Charlus's gros "pétard," when the narrator describes the male customers "accroupis comme des sphinx," rear ends exposed and at the ready. But while the grandmother is inside, the "marquise" discusses with a park attendent her clientele, in particular a magistrate of whom she is very proud. She continues: "Et puis . . . je choisis mes clients, je ne reçois pas tout le monde dans ce que j'appelle mes salons. Est-ce que ça n'a pas l'air d'un salon, avec mes fleurs?" (II, 606). And when a poorly dressed woman appears before the attendant "celle-ci, avec une férocité de snob, lui dit sèchement: 'il n'y a rien de libre, madame.' " Later, the grandmother tells Marcel she overheard the conversation, saying: "C'était on ne peut plus Guermantes et petit noyau Verdurin. Dieu! qu'en termes galants ces choses-là étaient mises" (II, 607).

From this analogy emerges the clear equation water=motherhood=homosexuality. Brichot implies that this water is dangerous when he explains that "mer voulait dire marais, comme dans . . . Cambremer" (III, 328), another etymology not found in the dictionaries Proust used. And because the salon/*maison de passe* is a matriarchal arena, it is no surprise that Proust links it to water, traditional symbol of femaleness. His exploitation of the homophones *mer/mère* is already a prime example of this technique and one which underscores as well the association of motherhood and lesbianism: the woman who seeks to repeat her relationship directly rather than vicariously with the preoedipal mother chooses a narcissistic rather than anaclitic love object. She chooses another woman. Thus, in the Proustian world lesbian activity systematically occurs near water. Joan Rosasco points out that in the course of his inquiry into Albertine's lesbianism, the narrator discovers that she used to go bathing with a laundress and friends at the Nice seaside or along the Loire in Touraine. "Il semble donc y avoir une sorte de progression logique selon laquelle cette eau se féminise jusqu'à rejoindre assez paradoxalement la mer" (72-84). To my mind, of course, there is no paradox. Quite the contrary, the feminization of water and its culmination in the *mer/mère* is an express pattern. Indeed, virtually all of Albertine's lesbian activities are somehow connected to water: Marcel first suspects this sexual preference at Balbec; Albertine's travels with Mlle Vinteuil's companion were to take her to Cherbourg or Holland; in Venice, the narrator wonders if his former mistress had had a lesbian relationship there when the hotel register reveals the name of the Baronne de Putbus who is allegedly associated with lesbianism; and when the narrator realizes that the lesbian activity he first observed in Combray has infiltrated his personal experience of women, the small pond or *mare* of Montjouvain expands exponentially to become a *mer:* "... derrière la plage de Balbec, *la mer* ... je voyais, avec des mouvements de désespoir. . .la chambre de Montjouvain . . ." (III, 513-14—emphasis added).

Indeed, the narrator ultimately blames Mother for the separation of the sexes and that is why Mme Verdurin reigns supreme at the end of *La Recherche*. The most perverse picture of motherhood possible, she promotes homosexuality. Not only was she linked intimately to Odette and did she encourage the Charlus/Morel tie, but by the novel's close La Patronne is in some way related to all the major characters who have swerved from heterosexuality. As the Princesse de Guermantes, she is the aunt of both Gilberte and Saint-Loup and connected to Andrée, eventually married to her nephew Octave. Furthermore, the stars of her salon are Morel and Rachel whose resemblance visually captures the hermaphrodite, source, not of convergent, but of divergent sexes that Proustian motherhood produces:

> Loin de réunir les sexes, il [l'hermaphrodite] les sépare, il est la source dont découlent continûment les deux séries homosexuelles divergentes, celle de Sodome et celle de Gomorrhe. C'est lui qui possède la clef de la prédiction de Samson: 'Les deux sexes mourront chacun de son côté'. (Deleuze 17-18)

Consequently, motherhood is excoriated through the condemnation of the water=motherhood=homosexuality equation. Proust not only collapses into one the *haut monde* and public restroom in his *marquise/toilettes* formula, but he also conflates high society and public baths in Albertine's supposed lesbian experience with a *doucheuse*. After all, the homonymy with *duchesse*, while not exact, is close enough. Both the marchioness-of-the-toilets and the duchess-of-the-showers are synonymous with waters sullied, in the first case, by someone washing the body of exterior dirt and, in the second, by someone cleansing the body of interior waste.[1] Ultimately then, motherhood is equated with impurities and excrement.

No one makes this analogy between motherhood and excrement better than Charlus, for as several duchesses comment after the musical evening in Mme Verdurin's home, the baron could throw a party in a "cabinet de toilettes" and it would not be any less remarkable (III, 777). Earlier, at a reception in the first Princesse de Guermantes's home, Charlus responds to the question of whether he will be attending Mme de Saint-Euverte's party—she's within earshot—by saying that such a question is like asking him if he has diarrhea. He would try to relieve himself elsewhere, he says, and adds, "On me dit que l'infatigable marcheuse donne des 'garden-parties' moi j'appellerais ça 'des invites à se promener dans les égoûts'. Est-ce que vous allez vous crotter là?" (III, 99). Moreover, he explains high society to Morel in the following manner:

> Quant à tous les petits messieurs qui s'appellent marquis de Cambremerde ou de Fatefairefiche, il n'y a aucune différence entre eux et le dernier pioupiou de votre régiment. Que vous alliez faire pipi chez la comtesse Caca, ou caca chez la baronne Pipi, c'est la même chose, vous aurez compromis votre réputation et pris un torchon breneux comme papier hygiénique. Ce qui est malpropre. (III, 475-76)

Here the baron makes explicit the Mother/excrement equation that was hinted at in an earlier conversation between the Duchesse de Guermantes (then the Princesse des Laumes) and Swann. Thinly veiling her dislike of the younger Mme de Cambremer (Legrandin's sister), Oriane remarks that this family name is quite astonishing. "Il finit juste à temps, mais il finit mal!" (I, 335), she laughs, giving the words *mère*—because of its homonymy with *mer* and *merde* the same negative weight. Swann, for his part, comments that the name doesn't begin any better than it ends, suggesting that someone quite angry but also very proper didn't dare finish the

---

[1] There is a curious passage in which one of the Grand Hôtel employees, a "chasseur louche," tells the narrator that his sister has become a grande dame. He goes on to say that an activity she particularly delights in with her new status is leaving feces in a hotel room or a carriage she has occupied.

first word of the name. Certainly this is a reference to Général Cambronne who, according to the famous Waterloo anecdote, rebuffed an English officer with the epithet hinted at in the last syllable. However, "le mot de Cambronne" aside, it seems to me that Proust's use of homophony permits an additional interpretation more pertinent to this study—although admittedly less amusing than the "liftier's" Camembert. Cambremer appears to be another textual echo of the Combray *mère*.

There are a variety of reasons to make this comparison. First of all both the narrator's mother and Mme de Cambremer have roots in Combray. Each woman has an older counterpart, in the first case the narrator's grandmother and in the second case the dowager Mme de Cambremer, whom, in fact, Legrandin's sister frequently calls "ma mère." And it is with both of these elderly women that Marcel has most contact in Balbec. As for the two younger women, each has one son who markedly takes after the maternal side of the family and who eventually becomes a writer. Furthermore, the Cambremer male is a homosexual, information supported by a supposed affair with Saint-Loup and confirmed by the *Gaulois*-reading "sous-maîtresse" of the Maineville Palace and Charlus—serving as yet another subtle hint at the narrator's own inversion. Indeed, I suspect that the young Cambremer had what would have been for the narrator and Proust alike a marriage made in heaven. His bride Mlle d'Oloron, Jupien's niece and Charlus's adopted daughter, not only brought a considerable fortune to the recently impoverished Cambremer family, but she also offered easy access to the Guermantes, coveted by the Cambremer women. Finally, she had the grace to die of typhoid only a few weeks after the wedding ceremony, leaving her homosexual husband (that the baron deemed the best kind) free to pursue his sexual preference without the accomodations to a wife that limited Saint-Loup.

Most important, the portrait of the two Mmes de Cambremer, like those of the mother and grandmother, ultimately collapse into one and leave the impression that each contains resonances of the Combray mother. Thus, it is not insignificant that the first name of the younger Mme de Cambremer is Renée, the *Combray mère renaît*—the Combray mother is reborn. And Oriane's mean-spirited description of the woman reminds readers of the female behind the fictional mother: the duchess describes a "grosse femme," or worse, an "énorme herbivore" who is both an anglophile—she spoke about a recent trip to the British Museum—and somewhat pretentious in her use of language.

Both women's music appreciation, while it is reminiscent of the narrator's grandmother, also signals a comparison to Mme Verdurin. And it is only appropriate that the woman who is the epitome of repudiated motherhood should be tied to Mme de Cambremer, Combray *mère*. First of all, of some interest is the fact that Mme de Cambremer rents La Raspelière to Mme Verdurin, her seaside home in Balbec, once again privileging the significance of place. Yet of most importance is the manner in which, because of the similarity to Swann's dream, the older Mme de Cambremer physically transforms herself into Mme Verdurin. What marked La Patronne's metamorphosis was not only an elongated nose but a sprouting mustache. If the dowager has one outstanding physical attribute it is a hairy upper lip. During an impromptu visit to the beach the narrator describes a woman whose "yeux brillèrent . . . et sa poitrine huma l'air de la mer . . . Je crus qu'elle allait poser sur ma joue ses lèvres moustachues" (III, 212). Clearly this is the Mother held in horror, in contrast to the former feminine ideal, from whom the narrator now abhors the possibility of a kiss. This echo from Swann's dream demonstrates that what Mme Verdurin and Mme de Cambremer, the Combray *mère*, have most in common is their role as omnipotent phallic or preoedipal mother.

That Proust should excoriate this powerful Mother by equating her with human waste is not unusual. According to Dinnerstein, because humans, unable "to reconcile the delights of the flesh with its anguishes, its victories with its mortifications," avoid this task by assigning untainted humanness to man and the body's "mucky, humbling limitations" to the "goddess of the nursery" (133). Furthermore, Proust respects this dichotomy. All of his great artists—Bergotte, Vinteuil and Elstir—are men while the one exceptional female artist, Berma, because she is an actress, seems simply to exploit what comes naturally to the author's females. Women, such as Elstir's Gabrielle, can inspire or they can interpret like Mlle Vinteuil's companion, but never are they creators themselves. Similar to Berma, they are vehicles for the true artist. Noteworthy are the artists under La Patronne's tutelage—the pianist Dechambre, the violinist Morel and the sculptor Ski—who remain mediocre, unrecognized. In contrast, Elstir, an early "fidèle" known as Biche or Tiche, escapes the *petit noyau* and becomes one of *La Recherche*'s great talents, although Mme Verdurin sees things otherwise: "Du jour où il a quitté le petit noyau, ça a été un homme fini. Il paraît que mes dîners lui faisaient perdre du temps, que je nuisais au développement de son *génie,* dit-elle sur un ton d'ironie. Comme si la fréquentation d'une femme comme moi pouvait ne pas être salutaire à un artiste!" (III, 334). But that is Proust's message: to move into the masculine realm of culture and society a man must extricate himself from Nature, from the omnipotent preoedipal mother.

This attempt to get away from Nature, from contaminated female flesh, results in a fascination with death (Dinnerstein 136), and not surprisingly, Proust arranges the Mother's. When the Duc and Duchesse de Guermantes refuse to forgo a long-awaited masked ball in order to visit a dying relative, the novelist uses the unforgettable episode to enhance their shallowness and expose them for the reprehensible people they are. However, that the family member is Amanien d'Osmond whose nickname is Mama is no small matter. Arriving at the Princesse de Guermantes's home in his Louis XI costume, the duke is asked, "Mais vous ignorez donc que le pauvre Mama est à l'article de la mort?" (III, 61). His death becomes a reality shortly thereafter. Too close to the French *maman* to go unnoticed and immediately associated with the Mother in English—a language which Proust knew and uses in *La Recherche*—it seems that an unusual death penalty is levied against the mother. It is she who, by virtue of her preoedipal influence, prevents mutual love between the sexes and encourages Marcel's view of love which precludes community and "implies that there is really nothing but masturbation" (Nussbaum, 505).

Indeed, when the narrator recounts, as is so often the case, a seemingly benign anecdote about childhood friends, he appears to say that the only route to heterosexuality necessarily excludes the Mother. The two friends, who meet again after many years, recall their puerile quasi-homosexual romps in the grass. Shortly thereafter one leaves for what is described as an arduous and virile horseback ride. The friend left behind reflects on his own homosexuality and compares himself to the other man, viewing him as "émancipé, à tant de milliers de mètres au-dessus de niveau de la *mer*" (III, 26—emphasis added). In fact, this statement bears a curious resemblance to one that Swann makes and which, moreover, resonates with the dream in which, walking beside the *mer/mère,* he sees himself castrated by the phallic mother, Mme Verdurin. Angered by her visible preference for Forcheville, he decides to distance himself from La Patronne, instinctively safeguarding his sexuality at the same time: "J'habite à trop de milliers de mètres d'altitude au-dessus des bas-fonds où clapotent et clabaudent de tels sales papotages, pour que je puisse être éclaboussé par les plaisanteries d'une Verdurin" (I, 282). (Swann also particpates in the Mother/feces analogy when he describes a trip to the country Odette takes with Mme Verdurin as a visit to the latrine to smell the excrement [I, 288].) As for the narrator, and Proust as well, he will never achieve this emancipation and returns to the sea—thus, to the Mother—for an image which subtly suggests his own homosexuality:

> Méduse! Orchidée! Quand je ne suivais que mon instinct, la méduse me répugnait à Balbec; mais si je savais la regarder, comme Michelet, du point de vue de l'histoire naturelle et de l'esthétique, je voyais une délicieuse girandole d'azur. Ne sont-elles pas, avec le velours transparent de leurs pétales, comme les mauves orchidées de la mer? (III, 28)

Although the narrator insists throughout *A la recherche du temps perdu* on his own heterosexual orientation, many critics contradict this claim. J. E. Rivers builds his case around the hero's personality traits which correspond to a turn-of-the-century description of homosexual temperament: Marcel is sickly and neurasthenic; he lacks willpower; he is preoccupied with masturbation; and Tante Léonie privileges a heredity which might cause sexual perversion in another generation (208-09). Alain Buisine finds a homosexual narrator in Proust's onomastic technique. In the pseudonym Charmel that Charlus wants to give Charles Morel, he finds a contraction of Marcel and Charlus, in other words a Marcel adept at "charlisme" (77). Eve Kosofsky Sedgwick makes a persuavive case for the narrator as closeted homosexual in a novel which simultaneously demands and forbids this violence against Marcel which would expose his closet as spectacle (223). And Ghislaine Florival states quite simply that the novel's meaning *must* be read in conjunction with an understanding of Proust's experience. The narrator cannot be disassociated from the novelist or his fictional substitutes (247), Swann among them, of course, but also Charlus.

To my mind, though, Marcel indicates his own inversion when he admits this new found admiration for the *méduse,* or jellyfish, a hermaphroditic organism where male and female sexual organs coexist separately. (Interestingly enough, Darwin found that the sea (*mer/mère*) privileges hermaphroditic organisms in a way that the earth does not [Miguet 556].) Not only does this hermaphrodite belie the narrator's heterosexuality, but the very word *méduse* does so as well. It necessarily brings to mind the legendary gorgon whose head Freud sees as a figure for female genitals which, moreover, quash all sexual rapprochement. In a note when citing Ferenczi, his contemporary to whom he owed this analogy, the psychoanalyst adds: ". . . what is indicated in the myth is the *mother's* genitals. Athene (*sic*), who carries Medusa's head on her armour, becomes in consequence the unapproachable woman, the sight of whom extinguishes all thought of sexual approach" (144, n. 3). Appropriately enough, Marcel himself points up this same equivalence when, after establishing throughout the novel this compellingly significant homonymy between *mer/ mère,* he ultimately says of *les méduses:* "Ne sont-elles pas, avec le velours transparent de leurs pétales, comme les mauves orchidées de la mer?"

In fact, the Medusa legend lends itself to interesting Proustian parallels and, supported by an object relational reading of *La Recherche,* reveals the text to be a cathartic confrontation with the novelist's sexual preference, offering a plausible explanation of Marcel's inversion which moves beyond the well-worn Oedipus Complex. Greek mythology recounts that it is Perseus who slays the gorgon and presents her head to Athena. And it is, in truth, Athena who is responsible for this creature: when the graceful maiden that was once Medusa attempted to rival Athena's beauty, the goddess (for whom Minerva is another name) stripped her of her charms, turning her lovely hair into hissing snakes and making the Medusa so frightening a sight that anyone who looked at her was turned to stone. Perseus assumed the task of slaying the Medusa to liberate Seriphus, a country ravaged by the monster. More significant, however, is the personal history which equips Perseus singularly well for the murder of this maternal equivalent. An oracle had told his grandfather Acrisius that Perseus would some day kill him, and as a consequence, his grandfather had Perseus and his mother enclosed in a box and set adrift at sea. Certainly this claustrophobic relationship to the Mother and potential fear of the sea (personified, many scholars theorize, by the gorgons [Bulfinch 96]) coincides with that of Marcel who was also (so to speak) boxed in with the Mother and an easy victim to the terrors of the sea—of the *Mer/Mère.*

As I have already suggested, Marcel never appears to move beyond primary union with the Mother, and his Mother as Mirror, used to organize the child's cohesive being, is clearly the Medusa, that is to say, sight of her literally petrifies the spectator. But the Medusa contains a double message. By refusing female genitalia, the narrator implies that a male sex, a phallus easily visible in either the tentacles of the jellyfish or the Medusa's serpents, is what he seeks. Thus the juxtaposition of the desired male and repugnant female sex gives way to a male/female opposition between the *méduse* and the *orchidées de la mer*. Yet the *orchidées de la mer* alone capture this dichotomy because they resonate with the estranged male and female orchids of the Guermantes courtyard that need an intermediary for fertilization. Moreover, the possessive *de la mer* suggests that the Mother is the third party in this triangle, and indeed, she who, through the power of her possessiveness, seals their fate. However, as Sedgwick points out, there is a curious contradiction in the analogy drawn between these flowers and the Charlus/Jupien coupling. The reader is meant to understand "how unlikely fulfillment is, of how absurdly, impossibly specialized and difficult is the need of each" (220), and yet this is evidently not the case. This male couple is "the single exception to every Proustian law of desire, jealousy, triangulation, and radical epistemological instability" (220). They need no go-between and, in choosing the same-sex love object, can forgo the Mother's mediation. Consequently, while Sedgwick sees the botanical hermaphrodism as a red herring that does nothing to clarify or deepen the model of sexual inversion, I find its contrast to the heterosexual couple an essential key to understanding Jupien and Charlus, and ultimately the narrator.

It is Albertine, of course, who uncovers the full meaning of the *Mère/Méduse* and whose extraordinary head of hair even seems to capture the affective difference, changing from a "couronne bouclée de violettes noires" (III, 528) to "cheveux hirsutes" (III, 862). It is the Mother, however, that Marcel decides to castigate, certainly for those earlier sins of possessiveness (the extensive preoedipal period) and selfish indifference (the asymmetry of their relationship). But most of all the narrator, and Proust, wish to punish this "mer que nous essayons ridiculement, comme Xerxès, de battre pour la punir" for her separation of the sexes, "de ce qu'elle a englouti" (III, 612). The Mother, the charming creature that was once the Medusa herself, becomes the reptile-crowned gorgon. Proust appears expressly to use the grandmother, synonymous with Nature and initially the most admired of the female characters, to visualize this metamorphosis. Appropriately enough on her deathbed, she submits to Cottard's final efforts to save her, a bloodletting that requires leeches all over her head. Marcel enters her room and sees "les petits serpents noirs [qui] se tordaient dans sa chevelure ensanglantée, comme dans celle de Méduse" (II, 630). Thus, comparable to Perseus who beheaded the monster, Marcel cuts the Mother down to size: "Qu'y a-t-il de plus poétique que Xerxès, fils de Darius, faisant fouetter de verges la mer . . .?" (III, 556). On the other hand, the *pine* of the novel's early pages, of Combray, has assumed, I would like to suggest, its full size as *verge,* and the narrator chastens the Mother by menacing her with his choice of same-sex love object.

Maternal blame, it seems to me, is indisputable. First of all, when the narrator reminisces about the Combray *scène du coucher,* he regretfully comments: "Si j'avais osé maintenant, j'aurais dit à maman: 'Non je ne veux pas, ne couche pas ici'" (I, 38). On the other hand, at the close of Combray, this memorable night a *fait accompli,* the profaning of Vinteuil's portrait resembles the blaspheming of Mme Jeanne Proust's photo. And the interchangeability of Vinteuil and Proust's mother points the way to the similarity between Mlle Vinteuil and Proust/narrator, metamorphosing the men into the same "sadique" and "artiste du mal" (I, 162) capable of using the novel as an instrument of profanation. Indeed, Doubrovsky has long argued that it is more appropriate, rather than the "jeunes filles en fleurs," to discuss the "fleurs du mal" of *La Recherche.* That blasphemy of the Mother should be captured by a lesbian couple is wholly appropriate since exclusion from a feminine sexual economy is what triggers Marcel's repudiation. For Proust, Mother is dead and he can give full reign to his animosity.

Sedgwick would reproach me this blame, all the while admitting the essential role of the Mother to whom this "coming-out testament and its continued refusal to come out are addressed" (248). Although the omnipotent yet unknowing mother is frequently a figure of literary production, deeply entrenched in twentieth-century gay male high culture, rarely is it at issue in gay male criticism and theory because of the potential indictment of motherhood. According to Sedgwick it would appear to support "unthinking linkages between (homo) sexuality and (feminine) gender" and to reinforce "the homophobic insistence, popularized from Freudian sources with astonishing effect by Irving Bieber and others in the fifties and sixties, that mothers are to be 'blamed' for—always unknowingly—causing their sons' homosexuality" (249). But Sedgwick shrugs off a helpful ally when she dismisses psychoanalytic theory, in particular object relations theory. It points out the pitfalls of parenting to relieve the Mother of blame, to show that it is the dynamics of childrearing in the present bourgeois model that is suspect. This theory indicts the system which places all the child care tasks on women and, thus, holds them responsible for a child's sexuality, even though it would never claim that this relationship alone is the source of sexual preference. The narrator's repudiation of the Mother is simply the symptom of this system.

Indeed, deceived by the Mother, the narrator reverses Freud's formula for heterosexual relations. Instead of choosing someone modeled on the Mother and opposite to himself, an anaclitic love object, he becomes the Mother himself, a role he sometimes assumed with Albertine: "Car quelquefois, en train de faire l'homme sage quand je parlais à Albertine, il me semblait entendre ma grand-mère" (III, 615). However, this time he chooses someone like him, a narcissistic love object, a strategy Ronald Hayman feels Proust used himself (40). Here Marcel seems, as he did in his preoedipal relationship with the Mother, to follow what has been traditionally deemed a female course of development. Similar to the author, the narrator appears more interested in *being* loved than in loving, for this is what has been inevitably missing in his relationships beyond that with the Mother. He would like to imitate what excludes him from the lesbian world, female narcissistic self-sufficiency, for he envies her her inaccessible libidinal position. She has kept her original narcissism intact while he has emptied himself of it to the advantage of the love object. Through his own inversion Marcel plans on rectifying the situation.

Finally, like Perseus, who not only frees Seriphus but himself as well with the Medusa's death, Marcel sees repudiation of the Mother as his own liberation. In writing his novel—indeed, an activity that Proust did not begin until the Mother's death—he extricates himself from the omnipotent preoedipal Mother and moves into the masculine economy of culture and society. By transforming the Mother into the Medusa, the narrator reveals the potential horrors of the *Mer/Mère,* the original non-self which threatens formation of the I and who can always lure others back into non-being "to engulf, dissolve, drown, suffocate them as autonomous persons" (Dinnerstein 112). Thus, again like Perseus, who knew that looking into the Medusa's gaze would turn him to stone, Marcel ultimately turns away from the Mother to avoid petrification, to escape being *médusé,* for a return to oneness with the Mother is a menace to selfhood.

A la recherche du temps perdu becomes a working through of Marcel's (Proust's) desire to return to primary union with the Mother. Florival notes:

> C'est que le retentissement vécu prolonge *le passé affectif dont l'adulte n'a jamais pu se détacher.* Sa vie n'est qu'un *perpétuel retour aux sources,* dans une sorte de réseau fermé à toute transcendance. Elle est prise aux reflets du moi dans les choses et les êtres perçus, dans la *répétition obsessionnelle,* impitoyable du désir inverti. Car choses et personnes ne sont que l'image du souvenir et s'intègrent dans le champ narcissique du moi. (125—emphasis added)

As Florival points out later, if the narrator (Proust) is going to fulfill himself it will not be in an "amour réconcilié" (220)—in a relationship where mother and mistress are collapsed into one and reciprocal love succeeds—but rather he shall accomplish this in the masterpiece itself where he can at least confront and work through his relations with the Mother. "D'autre part, l'oeuvre se donne comme le fruit d'une sorte de thérapeutique, de *catharsis,* mais à la manière d'une autoanalyse en relation avec telle ou telle réminiscence (Combray, Montjouvain, et la reconnaissance du 'meurtre' de la mère)" (21). Comparable to Marcel's first piece of writing, his description of the Martinville belltowers that had so perfectly relieved him of their being and "ce qu'ils cachaient derrière eux" (I, 180), the novel will serve the same purpose for his relationship with the Mother.

Thus while homosexual love may be biologically sterile, for Proust it is the wellspring of intellectual richness. In fact, Rivers feels that *La Recherche* owes its very existence to homosexual history and inspiration (138). However, I would emphasize, instead, the Mother, for people spend their life asserting themselves against the first parent with a vengeance (Dinnerstein 174), and this novelist is among the most egregious examples. I disagree that sexuality is out of control and that it in no way structures the novel (Rivers 18). Quite the contrary. Proust, in an interview published in *Le Temps* on November 12, 1913 (eight years after his mother's death), said that he had written a group of "novels of the Unconscious" (Bersani 212), and they, indeed, do contain the psychological unity of a dream (Bersani 243). The Mother, Kofman points out, "Loin d'être la figure d'une spontanéité sans interdit, elle représente la loi et la nécessité: celle du temps, de la Mort, de la *différence*" (88). Ultimately, the narrator (Proust) triumphs over the Mother. His struggle and eventual inability to overcome difference—the exclusive world of the feminine whose foremost sign is the Mother—propels the novel forward, and it is the novel which allows him to escape both Time and Death. Indeed, the most famous Mother of all, Mary, serves as a guide in his attempt at parthenogenesis, his only remaining option, to bring another immortal into the world.

Conclusion

The unflattering image of femininity which consumes all others by the novel's close begs for an explanation of why feminists instinctively admire Proust. Ostensibly, the concluding portrait of reprehensible motherhood precludes such admiration, but I would suggest it is, instead, its key. As Christiane Olivier points out, "Full existence for women depends on a prior desacralizing of the mother, whose long reign has given rise to misogyny in men and jealousy in women" (147). At an unconscious level women (along with the narrator and Proust) enjoy this castigation of motherhood because of their frustrating interpenetration with the Mother. No other text so clearly demonstrates the infelicitous results of maternal power than *A la recherche du temps perdu*.

Ultimately, Proust proves Mme de Villeparisis right: the emblematic mother-child relationship between Mme de Sévigné and Mme de Grignan *does* "manque de naturel." By altering their experiences to meet an ideal—fictionalized, the two women live in unflagging harmony while in life things were far more rocky—Proust imitates Oriane de Guermantes's ploy and says the opposite of what he wishes understood. Nothing preordains the natural mother and her child as a problem-free union marked by mutual love. The novelist suggests other parent-child possibilities, and in fact, once the narrator leaves Combray the traditional family runs amuck. Caretakers are infrequently a biological parent (Mme Bontemps or Mme de Villeparisis) nor is the primary parent always a woman (M. Vinteuil). Nevertheless, there is an overriding paternal absence, and it by no means lets fathers off the hook but demonstrates instead the deleterious effects of such a vacuum. Indeed, because the novel so adeptly illustrates the hazards of female primacy in parenthood it can be seen as a cautionary tale which forecasts the argument for different parenting patterns that Chodorow and Dinnerstein make more than fifty years later.

Equally as interesting for feminist readers is how many of Proust's women reject conventional roles, although this phenomenon prompts other readers to dismiss these females as males in disguise: "The parts of the novel which depict girls and women in rebellion against traditional female roles . . . shatter stereotypes and challenge some of the most fundamental assumptions of Western culture. That is why these sections have been denounced and rejected as unconvincing . . ." (Rivers 244). But it is not simply Gilberte making an obscene gesture or Albertine, unmarried, living with the narrator which suggests rebellion. It is also the female psychological stance. Indeed, when it comes to femininity, Proust, so frequently cited as someone who unwittingly reinforces Freud, contradicts a variety of Freudian notions. Penis-envy is stood on its head in a text where men envy women, because of their libidinal position of seeming self-satisfaction, and not the other way round. The novelist's females ultimately inhabit a closed universe and their inaccessibility makes them all the more tantalizing to men. By virtue of their many metamorphoses the women of *La Recherche* are in no way the immutable beings Freud believed they all became by the age of thirty. And ultimately numerous Proustian women refuse to assume the role of the good mother that the psychoanalyst wanted to impose on every female.

Here lies their most significant resistance. Proustian women seem to understand instinctively that to accept the good mother role is to perpetuate the imbalance of asymmetrical adult sexual relations. Although at first glance Proust's view of heterosexual love can be interpreted as overly pessimistic and the product of a cynical homosexual incapable of understanding heterosexual relations, a feminist reading of the text reveals the asymmetry which results when both partners are looking for the Mother. Marcel is not alone in this pursuit. Many of the novel's women participate in the very same exercise and demonstrate how their triangulation of the oedipal situation motivates them to take the Father as a love object but never to give up the Mother. Albertine hesitates between her attachment to the narrator and a maternal presence that her lesbian lifestyle permits. The antagonisms which exist between mothers and daughters are explained by both females' attempt at a balancing act between nurturance and autonomy. Gilberte de Saint-Loup, struggling for independence, may be embarrassed by Odette's presence at her high society receptions, but on the other hand, she understands that it was her mother's machinations that privileged her present position.

Like Marcel, Proustian women hope to "have it all." Just as he, not wanting to choose between Mother and Lover, hopes to reconcile the two, the females of *La Recherche* seek a similar both/and construct. They wish to be both the desired object and the valued subject, and they understand that heterosexual relations which demand of them—and not of men—monogamy, intimacy and sexuality framed strictly by the other's desire will never permit this. Thus they turn to an all female world where both partners can easily play each role of Mother and Lover. Built on the composer's suffering over his daughter (Swann asks himself: "au fond de quelles douleurs avait-il puisé cette force de dieu, cette puissance illimitée de créer?" [I, 342]), Vinteuil's sonata wafts through *La Recherche* as much a constant reminder of lesbianism as it is the "hymne national" of Swann and Odette's love. Because it brings to mind the beloved and, thus, her potential desire for another woman, it is the background music as women explode the notion of what Adrienne Rich calls compulsory heterosexuality and enter instead, whether by sexual relations or simple friendship, the lesbian continuum.

Indeed, because women's oppression ultimately turns on control of their sexuality, rebellious female sexuality is fundamental to understanding why Proust is the darling of feminists. By stressing women's primary bonds with other women—the real significance of the grandmother-mother relation—as well as the difficulties between men and women, the author undercuts several heterosexist assumptions. Not only does he question the naturalness of women alone as primary caretakers as well as the perfect reciprocity of heterosexual love, assumptions which temporarily dupe the narrator, but Proust also questions the seamless sexuality of any individual. He suggests that men and women alike are not of a piece but may be heterosexual at one stage in their life and homosexual at another: ". . . la nature que nous faisons paraître dans la seconde partie de notre vie n'est pas toujours, si elle l'est souvent, notre nature première développée ou flétrie, grossie ou atténuée; elle est quelquefois une nature inverse, un véritable vêtement retourné" (I, 426). It is even possible to suggest that those of his homosexual images which are stereotypical are meant, not to reinforce received views, but to expose them as silly. Charlus as a flaming queen renders ridiculous any reduction of inversion to such a portrait and simultaneously makes laughable certain behavior required of women. Furthermore, because Albertine possesses an orality that contrasts dramatically with Charlus's anality, schematized by active/passive or male/female and possibly seen as demeaned femininity, Albertine "could be seen to embody a modern, less mutilating and hierarchical sexuality even as she (or he) represented the more empowered 'New Woman' " (Sedgwick 237). Most important though, male jealousy at strong female bonds exposes the link between homophobia and patriarchy.

The narrator's jealousy, in the end, is tied to his frustration at being excluded from a universe which prompts reconciliation of Subject and Other. Femininity privileges the both/and construct, although many, most notably Rivers, would argue that it is androgyny which achieves this goal. And there is undoubtedly a blurring of gender boundaries in *La Recherche,* not unexpected from a writer who said he wanted in women "Des vertus d'homme" and in men "Des charmes féminins" (*Contre Sainte-Beuve,* 336). However, this incredulity in the face of strict gender categories has more to do with with the primary caretaker's influence than with innate androgyny. After all, Mme Jeanne Proust's dominion over her son favored his feminine nature, and as long as the Mother reigns supreme the feminization of females and males alike remains a real possibility. That Miss Sacripant is the "archetypal metaphor" of *La Recherche* (Rivers 231) seems to me true, not because of the androgyny of an Odette in male clothing but rather for the femininity which bodies forth in this text where so many others see nothing but men. The two homosexual desires have but one thing in common: they lean toward the feminine. Albertine and Charlus alike are feminized by their inversion, that is to say, they move towards a female space which represents the unknowable (Sedgwick 234). In contrast to Rivers who sees androgyny as the creative force behind the novel, I see the narrator's struggle to enter a feminine economy as one of its major inspirations and agree with Serge Doubrovsky when he says that what Marcel really wants is to be a woman.

But, of course, he never quite succeeds. Blurred boundaries are all that is possible, as the novel's opening pages announce—". . . il me semblait que j'étais moi-même ce dont parlait l'ouvrage: une église, un quatuor, la rivalité de François Ier et de Charles Quint" (I, 3). The narrator remains as firmly within the separate confines of Sodom and Gomorrha as does every character of *A la recherche du temps perdu,* for they do not simply represent homosexuals but heterosexuals as well. In the first instance the two groups have no sexual interest in one another, and in the second, while the interest is there, sexual assymetry keeps men and women apart. Marcel settles on the *méduse* over the *orchidées de la mer,* refuses self-hatred and assumes his homosexuality. Sodom and Gomorrha are the very essence of the masterpiece's spiritual fecundity. Proust illustrates as well as anyone the feminist notion that gender ineluctably influences the creative process—and this can easily have nothing to do with sex.

Bibliography

Adam, A. "Le personnage de Proust et le problème des clés." *La Revue des Sciences Humaines* 65 (1952): 49-90.

Alberti, Frank and Yvonne Marsigné. "Les deux 'courrières' de Balbec visitées." *Bulletin de la Société des Amis de Marcel Proust* 23 (1973): 1574-86.

Amer, Henry. "Littérature et portrait: Retz, Saint-Simon, Chateaubriand et Proust." *Etudes françaises* 3 (1967): 131-68.

Appignanesi, Lisa. *Femininity and the Creative Imagination: A Study of Henry James, Robert Musil and Marcel Proust.* London: Vision, 1973.

Bader, Clarisse. *La femme française.* Paris: Perrin, 1885.

Bardèche, Maurice. *Marcel Proust, romancier.* 2 vols. Paris: Les Sept Couleurs, 1971.

Barthes, Roland. *Michelet par lui-même.* Paris: Seuil, 1954.

Bataille, Georges. *La littérature et le mal.* Paris: Gallimard, 1957.

———. "Marcel Proust et la mère profanée." *Critique* 47 (1946): 601-11.

Beckett, Samuel. *Proust.* New York: Grove Press, 1931.

Bell, Clive. *Proust.* New York: Harcourt, Brace and Company, 1929.

Bellemin-Noël, Jean. *Psychanalyse et littérature.* Paris: Presses Universitaires de France, 1978.

———. *Vers l'inconscient du texte.* Paris: Presses Universitaires de France, 1978.

Bérence, Fred. "Une héroïne de Proust. Souvenirs inédits sur la reine de Naples." *Nouvelles littéraires* (26 septembre 1946).

Bergler, Edmund. "Proust and the 'torture-theory of love.'" *The American Image* 10 (1953): 265-88.

Berl, Emmanuel. "L'amour dans l'œuvre de Proust." *Preuves* 175 (1965): 26-36.

Bersani, Leo. *Marcel Proust: The Fictions of Life and Art.* New York: Oxford University Press, 1965.

Birn, Randi M. "Love and Communication: An Interpretation of Proust's Albertine." *French Review* 40 (1966-67): 221-28.

Bolle, Louis. *Les vues de la Raspelière, personnages et perspectives dans l'œuvre de Marcel Proust.* Neuchâtel: La Baconnière, 1965.

Bonan, Mireille. "La psychologie des domestiques chez Proust." *Bulletin de la Société des Amis de Marcel Proust* 14 (1958): 225-29.

Bonaparte, Marie. *Female Sexuality.* New York: International Universities Press, 1953.
Bondivienne, Louis. *L'Education de la femme.* Paris: Dupont, 1874.
Bonnet, Henri. *Deux études sur Marcel Proust.* Paris: Le Rouge et le Noir, 1928.
Bordier, Roger. "Sur Zola et Proust: l'esprit de famille, l'art et le réel." *Europe* 496-97: 218-28.
Borie, Jean. *Le tyran timide; le naturalisme de la femme au XIXe siècle.* Paris: Klincksieck, 1973.
Bové, Carol Mastrangelo. "Women and Society in Literature, or Reading Kristeva and Proust." *The Dalhousie Review* 64 (Summer 1984): 260-69.
Bowie, Malcolm. *Freud, Proust and Lacan.* Cambridge: Cambridge University Press, 1987.
Bourke, L.H. "Jealousy." *Culture* 19 (1958): 65-87.
Bragg, Mary et al., eds. *Lesbian Psychologies.* Urbana and Chicago: University of Illinois Press, 1987.
Brée, Germaine. *Marcel Proust and Deliverance from Time.* New Brunswick: Rutgers University Press, 1955.
———. *The World of Marcel Proust.* London: Chatto and Windus, 1967.
Brincourt, J. "La psychologie de Proust et ses contempteurs." *Bulletin de la Société des Amis de Marcel Proust* 13 (1963): 42-53.
Bronne, Carlo. *Les roses de cire.* Bruxelles: André de Rache, 1972.
Buisine, Alain. "Matronymies." *Littérature* 55 (mai 1984): 54-78.
Bulfinch, Thomas. *Bulfinch's Mythology.* New York: Random House, n. d.
Cabire, Emma. "La conception subjectiviste de l'amour chez Marcel Proust." *Nouvelle Revue Française* 20 (1973): 212-21.
Cattui, Georges. "Albertine retrouvée." *Adam International Review* 25 (1957): 80-84.
———. "Les clés des types et le clavier des thèmes chez Proust." *Le Point* 55-56 (1959): 41-54.
Chambers, Ross. *L'ange et l'automate. Variations sur le mythe de l'actrice de Nerval à Proust.* Paris: Lettres Modernes, 1971.
Chambon, M. *Le Livre des mères.* Paris: Librairie Blériot, 1900.
Charles-Roux, Edmonde, et al. *Elles, Héroïnes de romans, miroir de leur temps.* Paris: Les Editeurs Français Réunis, 1975.
Chasseguet-Smirgel. Janine. *La sexualité féminine.* Paris: Petite Bibliothèque Payot, 1964.
Chodorow, Nancy. *The Reproduction of Mothering: Psychoanalysis and the Sociology of Gender.* Berkeley and Los Angeles: University of California Press, 1978.
Clancier, Anne. *Psychanalyse et critique littéraire.* Toulouse: Privat, 1973.
Clark, Charles N. "Love and Time: The Erotic Imagery of Marcel Proust." *Yale French Studies* 11 (1953): 80-90.

Clarke, Gerald. *Capote*. New York: Simon and Schuster, 1988.
Colette. *The Pure and the Impure*. Trans. Herma Briffault. New York: Farrar, Strauss and Giroux, 1975.
Compagnon, Antoine. "Ce frémissement d'un cœur à qui on fait mal." *Nouvelle Revue de Psychanalyse* 33 (mars 1986): 117-39.
Crémieux, Benjamin. *Du côté de Marcel Proust*. Paris: Editions Lemarget, 1929.
———. "La psychologie de Proust." *La Revue de Paris* (15 octobre 1924): 838-61.
Curtius, Ernest. *Marcel Proust*. Paris: Les Editions de la Revue Nouvelle, 1928.
Dandieu, Arnaud. *Marcel Proust, sa révélation psychologique*. Paris: Firmin-Didot et cie., 1930.
Daudet, Charles. *Répertoire des personnages d' "A la recherche du temps perdu."* Paris: Gallimard, 1928.
Damon, Gene. *The Lesbian in Literature: A Bibliography*. Reno, Nevada: The Ladder, 1975.
De Jean, Joan E. *Fictions of Sappho 1546-1937*. Chicago: University of Chicago Press, 1989.
Deleuze, Gilles. *Proust et les signes*. Paris: Presses Universitaires de France, 1974.
Deutsch, Helene. *The Psychology of Women*. New York: Grune and Stratton, 1944.
Dezon-Jones, Elyane. "Death of My Grandmother/Birth of a Text." *Critical Essays on Marcel Proust*. Ed. and trans. Barbara J. Bucknall. Boston: Hall, 1987. 192-204.
Dinnerstein, Dorothy. *The Mermaid and the Minotaur: Sexual Arrangements and Human Malaise*. New York: Harper Colophon Books, 1977.
Doubrovsky, Serge. *La Place de la madeleine*. Paris: Mercure de France, 1974.
Duffner, Jean. *L'Œuvre de Marcel Proust. (Etudes médico-psychologiques)*. Paris: Amédée Legrand, 1931.
Durand, Gilbert. *Les Structures anthropologiques de l'imaginaire*. Paris: Bordas, 1969.
Fairbairn, W. R. D. *An Object-Relations Theory of the Personality:* New York: Basic Books, 1952.
Feuillerat, Albert. *Comment Marcel Proust a composé son roman*. New Haven: Yale University Press, 1934.
Finn, Michael R. "Proust et Dumas Fils: Odette et La Dame aux Camélias." *The French Review* 47 (1974): 528-42.
Flax, Jane. "The Conflict Between Nurturance and Autonomy in Mother-Daughter Relationships and Within Feminism." *Feminist Studies* 4 (1978): 171-87.
Fleurant, M. "La personne humaine selon Proust." *Bulletin de la Société des Amis de Marcel Proust* 23 (1973).
———. "La personne humaine selon Proust (fin)." *Bulletin de la Société des Amis de Marcel Proust* 24 (1974).

Florival, Ghislaine. *Le désir chez Proust: A la recherche du sens.* Louvain: Editions Nauwelaerts, 1971.

Forrester, Viviane. "Marcel Proust: Le texte de la mère." *Tel Quel* (78): 70-82.

Foster, Jeannette. *Sex Variant Women in Literature.* Baltimore: Diana Press, 1975.

Fowlie, Wallace. *Climate of Violence.* New York: MacMillan, 1967.

——. *Love in Literature: Studies in Symbolic Expression.* Blooomington: Indiana University Press, 1965.

——. *A Reading of Proust.* Gloucester, Mass.: Peter Smith, 1969.

Freud, Sigmund. *The Standard Edition of Complete Psychological Works of Sigmund Freud.* Ed. and trans. James Strachey. 24 vols. London: Hogarth Press, 1974.

'Child is being beaten, A': A Contribution to the Study of the Origin of Sexual Perversion. Vol. 17.

Contributions to the Psychology of Love. Vol. 11.
    I.   Special Type of Choice of Object Made by Men.
    II. On the Universal Tendency to Debasement in the Sphere of Love.
    III. The Taboo of Virginity.

Female Sexuality. Vol. 21.

Hysterical Phantasies and Their Relation to Bisexuality. Vol. 9.

Interpretation of Dreams, The. Vol. 4.

Introductory Lectures on Psycho-Analysis. Vols. 15-16.

Medusa's Head. Vol. 18.

Narcissism, On: An Introduction. Vol. 14.

Neurotic Mechanisms in Jealousy, Paranoia and Homosexuality. Vol. 18.

New Introductory Lectures on Psycho-Analysis. Vol. 22.

Observations on Transference—Love. Vol. 12.

Psychical Consequences of the Anatomical Distinctions between the Sexes, Some. Vol. 19.

Psychogenesis of a Case of Homosexuality in a Woman, The. Vol. 18.

Three Essays on the Theory of Sexuality. Vol. 7.

Gallop, Jane. "Reading the Mother Tongue: Psychoanalytic Feminist Criticism" in *The Trial(s) of Psychoanalysis.* Ed. Françoise Meltzer. Chicago: The University of Chicago Press, 1988.

——. *The Daughter's Seduction. Feminism and Psychoanalysis.* Ithaca: Cornell University Press, 1982.

Gardiner, Judith Kegan. "Mind Mother: Psychoanalysis and Feminism." in *Making a Difference: Feminist Literary Criticism.* Eds. Gayle Greene and Coppelia Kahn. London: Methuen, 1985. 113-45.

Gaultier, Jules de. *Le Bovarysme.* Paris: Mercure de France, 1921.

Genette, Gérard. *Figures II.* Paris: Editions du Seuil, 1969.

Gilbert, Sandra M. "Costumes of the Mind: Transvestism as Metaphor in Modern Literature." *Critical Inquiry* (Winter 1980): 391-417.

Gilbert, Sandra M. and Susan Gubar. "Forward into the Past: The Complex Female Affiliation Complex." *Historical Studies in Literary Criticism.* Ed. Jerome J. McGann. Madison: University of Wisconsin Press, 1985. 240-65.

Girard, René. *Mensonge romantique et vérité romanesque.* Paris: Grasset, 1961.

Glikin, Gloria. "The 'I' and 'She.' " *Adam International Review* (1966): 310-12.

Graham, Victor E. *The Imagery of Proust.* Oxford: Blackwell, 1966.

Granoff, Wladimir and François Perrier. *Le désir et le féminin.* Paris: Aubier Montaigne, 1979.

Gray-McDonald, Margaret. "Marcel's Ecriture Féminine." *Modern Fiction Studies* 34 (1988): 337-52.

Grier, Barbara. *The Lesbian in Literature.* Tallahassee: Naiad Press, 1986.

Gutwirth, Marcel. "Swann and the Duchess." *The French Review* 38 (1964-65): 143-51.

Hachez, Willy. "Chronologie et l'âge des personnages." *Bulletin de la Société des Amis de Marcel Proust* 6 (1956).

———. "Retouches." *Bulletin de la Société des Amis de Marcel Proust* 13 (1961).

Hale, Jane Alison. "Le Théâtre de Guermantes." *Modern Language Studies* 15 (1985): 208-24.

Harris, Bertha. "Their More Profound Nationality of Their Lesbianism: Lesbian Society in Paris in the 1920's." *Amazon Expedition: A Lesbian-Feminist Anthology.* Ed. Phyllis Birkley et al. Washington, N.J.: Times Change Press, 1973. 77-88.

Harris, Elaine. *L'approfondissement de la sensualité dans l'œuvre romanesque de Colette.* Paris: Nizet, 1973.

Harvey, W. J. *Character and the Novel.* London: Chatto and Windus, 1965.

Hayman, Ronald. *Proust: A Biography.* New York: Harper Collins, 1990.

Hindus, Milton. "The Pattern of Proustian Love." *New Mexico Quarterly* 21 (1951): 389-405.

Hirsch, Marianne. "Mothers and Daughters: Review Essay." *Signs* 7 (1981): 200-22.

Hoffman, Frederick John. *Freudianism and the Literary Mind.* Baton Rouge: Louisiana State University Press, 1957.

Horney, Karen. *Feminine Psychology.* New York: W.W. Norton, 1967.

Houston, J. P. "Literature and Psychology: The Case of Proust." *L'Esprit créateur* 5 (1965): 3-13.

Huas, Jeanine. *Les femmes chez Proust.* Paris: Hachette, 1971.

Irigaray, Luce. *Ce sexe qui n'en est pas un.* Paris: Les Editions de Minuit, 1974.

———. *Le corps-à-corps avec la mère.* Montréal: Les Editions de la Pleine Lune, 1981.

———. *L'Une ne bouge pas sans l'autre.* Paris: Les Editions de Minuit, 1979.

Jennings, L. Chantal. "L'amour-passion de Tristan à l'œuvre proustienne: vicissitudes d'un mythe." *Symposium* (1971): 123-37.

Johnson, Barbara. *The Critical Difference*. Baltimore: Johns Hopkins University Press, 1980.

Kahane, Claire. "Questioning the Maternal Voice." *Genders* 3 (November 1988): 82-91.

Kofman, Sarah. *L'énigme de la femme: La femme dans les textes de Freud*. Paris: Editions Galilée, 1980.

Kostis, Nicholas. "Albertine: Characterization through Image and Symbol." *PMLA* 84 (1969): 125-35.

Kristeva, Julia. "Stabat Mater." *Poetics Today* 6 (1985): 133-52.

Lacretelle, Jacques de. *Portraits d'autrefois et figures d'aujourd'hui*. Paris: Perrin, 1973.

Lassus, Jean de. "Marcel Proust et les psychologues du monde." *Le Divan* (mars 1973).

Laurent, M. "Explication française. Marcel Proust et l'amour: l'affaiblissement de l'amour." *L'Ecole* (13 mai 1961).

Lejeune, Philippe. "Ecriture et sexualité." *Europe* 49 (1971): 113-43.

Levin, Harry and Justin O'Brien. "Proust, Gide and the Sexes." *PMLA* 65 (1950): 648-53.

Levin, Harry. *The Gates of Horn*. New York: Oxford University Press, 1963.

Lotringer, Sylvie. "Proust polymorphe." *Poétique* 11 (1980): 170-76.

Lynes, Carlos. "Proust and Albertine: On the Limits of Autobiography and of Psychological Truth in the Novel." *Journal of Aesthetics and Art Criticism*, 10 (1952), 328-37.

Mann, Chris. "The Eclipse of Madame Putbus's Chambermaid in *A la recherche du temps perdu*." *New Zealand Journal of French Studies* 8 (1987): 25-33.

Marks, Elaine. "Lesbian Intertextuality." *Homosexualities and French Literature*. Ed. George Stambolian and Elaine Marks. Ithaca: Cornell University Press, 1979. 353-77.

Martinoir, Niane de. "Du temps des essences à l'illusion volontaire, ou la fonction des robes et des salons dans l'univers imaginaire de Marcel Proust." *Revue des Sciences Humaines* 143 (1971): 405-16.

Maurois, André. *A la recherche de Marcel Proust*. Paris: Hachette, 1949.

———. *Le monde de Marcel Proust*. Paris: Hachette, 1960.

———. *Sept visages de l'amour*. Paris: Jeune Parque, 1942.

Mein, Margaret. *A Foretaste of Proust: A Study of Proust and His Precursors*. London: Saxon House, 1974.

Miguet, Marie. "L'hermaphroditisme dans l'œuvre de Marcel Proust." *Bulletin de la Société des Amis de Marcel Proust* 32 (1982): 556-74.

———. "Un épisode de '*Sodome et Gomorrhe.*' Mme de Surgis et ses fils. Parthénogèse et hermaphroditisme." *Bulletin de la Faculté de Lettres de Mulhouse,* VI (1974), 51-57.

Miller, Jean Baker, M.D. *Toward a New Psychology of Women.* Boston: Beacon Press, 1986.

Miller, Milton L., M.D. *Nostalgia—A Psychoanalytical Study of Marcel Proust.* Boston: Houghton Mifflin, 1956.

Mitchell, Juliet. *Psychoanalysis and Feminism.* New York: Pantheon Books, 1974.

Montrelay, Michèle. *L'Ombre et le nom—sur la féminité.* Paris: Editions de Minuit, 1977.

Morice, Louis. "Un regard d'Odette." *L'Enseignement secondaire* 43 (1964): 171-76.

Muller, Marcel. "*Sodome I* ou la naturalisation de Charlus." *Poétique* 8 (1971): 470-78.

Nell-Boelsche, Sharon. "Nocturnal Agony and Diurnal Ecstasy in a Passage from *A la recherche du temps perdu.*" *West Virginia University Philological Papers* 31 (1986): 33-8.

Newman-Gordon, Pauline. *Dictionnaire des idées dans l'œuvre de Marcel Proust.* Paris: Mouton, 1968.

Nicolas, Louis. *Marcel Proust et la femme: Essai de critique médico-psychologique.* Bordeaux: Cadoret, 1931.

Nitzberg, Howard. "Du côté de chez Swann. The Orpheus and Euridice Theme." *Language Quarterly* XIV (1975): 15.

Nussbaum, Martha. "Love's Knowledge." *Perspectives on Self-Deception.* Ed. Brian P. McLaughlin. Berkeley: University of California Press, 1988. 487-514.

O'Brien, Justin. "Albertine the Ambiguous: Notes on Proust's Transposition of the Sexes." *PMLA* 44 (1949): 933-52.

Olivier, Christiane. *Jocasta's Children. The Imprint of the Mother.* Trans. George Craig. London and New York: Routledge, 1989.

Orlando, Walter. "Conversation avec Mme Verdurin." *Ecrits de Paris* (1968): 93-96.

Painter, George D. "The Duchess regained." *The New Statesman and Nation* 14 (February 1953) 186.

———. *Proust: The Early Years.* New York: Atlantic Little, Brown, 1959.

———. *Proust: The Later Years.* New York: Atlantic Little, Brown, 1965.

Pasco, Allan H. "Albertine's Equivocal Eyes." *Australian Journal of French Studies* 5 (1968): 157-262.

———. *The Color-Keys to "A la recherche du temps perdu."* Genève: Librairie Droz, 1976.

———. "Marcel, Albertine and Balbec in Proust's Allusive Complex." *Romanic Review* 62 (1971): 113-26.

Peyre, Henri, ed. *Baudelaire: A Collection of Critical Essays.* Englewood Cliffs, N.J.: Prentice-Hall, Inc., 1962.

Picard, Gaston. "Faut-il renier Freud et Proust?" *La Revue Mondiale* (1er décembre 1929): 343-67.

Pierre-Quint, Léon. *Comment travaillait Proust.* Paris: Editions des Cahiers Libres, 1928.

———. *Marcel Proust, sa vie, son œuvre.* Paris: Editions du Sagittaire, 1935.

Pifer, Mary Gayle. "L'Amour cyclique proustien." *Chimères* (printemps 1972): 1530.

Pigeot, Jacqueline. "Importance du personnage de Mme Verdurin dans *le Temps retrouvé.*" *Sevriennes d'hier et d'aujourd'hui* (mars 1966): 9-13.

Pluchart, Bernard. *Proust: l'amour comme vérité humaine et romanesque.* Paris: Larousse, 1975.

Ponse, Barbara. *Identities in the Lesbian World: The Social Construction of Self.* Westport, Connecticut: Greenwood Press, 1978.

Porché, François. *L'Amour qui n'ose pas dire son nom.* Paris: Grasset, 1927.

Pritchett, V. S. *Marcel Proust, comptes rendus.* Paris: Colin, 1971.

Proust, Marcel. *A la recherche du temps perdu.* Ed. Jean-Yves Tadié. 4 vols. Paris: Gallimard, Bibliothèque de la Pléiade, 1987.

———. *Contre Sainte-Beuve.* Paris: Gallimard, Bibliothèque de la Pléiade, 1971.

———. *Les Plaisirs et les Jours.* Paris: Gallimard, 1924.

Quémar, Claudine. "Rêverie(s) onomastique(s) proustienne(s) à la lumière des avant-textes." *Littérature* 28 (1977): 77-99.

Radovici, Nadia. "La vraie personnalité de Mlle Vinteuil." *Bulletin de la Société des Amis de Marcel Proust,* 23 (1973).

Renauld, Pierre. "Psychologie proustienne et conscience mythique." *Bulletin de la Société des Amis de Marcel Proust* 21 (1971): 1157-64; 22 (1972), 1398-1405.

Richard, Jean-Paul. *Proust et le monde sensible.* Paris: Editions du Seuil, 1974.

Rich, Adrienne. "Compulsory Heterosexuality and Lesbian Existence." *Blood, Bread and Poetry: Selected Prose, 1979-1985.* New York: W.W. Norton, 1986.

———. *Of Woman Born: Motherhood as Experience and Institution.* New York: W.W. Norton, 1977.

Rivers, J. E. *Proust and the Art of Love: The Aesthetics of Sexuality in the Life, Times, and Art of Marcel Proust.* New York: Columbia University Press, 1980.

Rivière, Jacques. *Quelques progrès dans l'étude du cœur humain (Freud et Proust).* Paris: Librairie de France, 1927.

Robert, Pierre-Edmond. "George Sand's Presence in Proust's *A la recherche du temps perdu.*" *West Virginia George Sand Conference Papers.* Ed. Armand E. Singer. Morgantown: Department of French WVU, 1981.

Robertson, Jane. "The Relationship between the Hero and Françoise in *A La Recherche*." *French Studies* 25 (1971): 437-41.
Roger, Alain. *Proust, les plaisirs et les noms*. Paris: Denoël, 1985.
Rosasco, J. "Aux Sources de la Vivonne." *Poétique* 7: 72-84.
Rosello, Mireille. "L'embonpoint du Baron de Charlus." *French Forum* 10 (1985): 189-200.
Ross, Kristin. "Albertine; or The Limits of Representation." *Novel* (1986): 135-49.
Rowland, Michael. "*Contre Sainte-Beuve* and Character Presentation in *A la recherche du temps perdu*." *Romance Notes* 8 (1967): 183-87.
Rule, Jane. *Lesbian Images*. Garden City, N. Y. : Doubleday, 1975.
Sagaert, Martine. "Marcel Proust et André Gide: L'Image biographique de la mère." *Revue des Sciences Humaines* 70 (1985): 107-30.
Schafer, Roy. "Problems in Freud's Psychology of Women." *Journal of the American Psychoanalytic Association* 22 (1974): 459-85.
Scott-Moncrieff, C. K., et al. *Marcel Proust, an English Tribute*. London: Chatto and Windus, 1923.
Sedgwick, Eve Kosofsky. *Epistemology of the Closet*. Berkeley and Los Angeles: University of California Press, 1990.
Simon, Pierre-Henri. "Psychologie proustienne de l'amour." *Hommes et Mondes* 44 (1950): 382-295.
Souza, Sybil de. "The Role of Odette de Crécy in *A la recherche du temps perdu*." *The Windmill* 2 (1946): 103-10.
Splitter, Randolph. *Proust's "Recherche": A Psychoanalytic Interpretation*. Boston: Routledge and Kegan Paul, 1981.
Sprengnether, Madelon. *The Spectral Mother. Freud, Feminism and Psychoanalysis*. Ithaca: Cornell University Press, 1990.
St. Laurent, Maureen E. "Albertine Asleep: Possession of Consciousness in *Remembrance of Things Past*." *Style* 22 (1988): 516-23.
Stockinger, Jacob. "Colette and Lesbians." *Colette: The Woman, The Writer*. Eds. Erica Mendelson Eisinger and Mary Ward McCarty. University Park and London: The Pennsylvania State University Press, 1981.
Stoller, Robert J. M.D. "Facts and Fancies: An Examination of Freud's Concept of Bisexuality" in *Women and Analysis*. Ed. Jean Strouse. New York: Grossman Publishers, 1974.
Suleiman, Susan. "Writing and Motherhood." In *The (M)other Tongue: Essays in Feminist Psychoanalytic Interpretation*. Edited by Shirley Nelson Garner, Claire Kahane and Madelon Sprengnether. Ithaca: Cornell University Press, 1985, pp. 352-77.

Sullivan, Dennis G. "On Theatricality in Proust: Desire and the Actress." *Modern Language Notes*, 86 (1971), 532-54.

Tupinier, Georgette. *Autour de cinq ébauches de Mlle de Stermaria*. Paris: Gallimard, 1973.

Van de Ghinste, J. *Rapports humains et communications dans "A la recherche du temps perdu."* Paris: Nizet, 1975.

Vernière, Paul. "Les jeunes filles chez Proust." *Revue de la Méditerranée* 17 (1957): 486-502.

Weinstein, Arnold L. *Vision and Response in Modern Fiction*. Ithaca: Cornell University Press, 1974.

Zéphir, Jacques J. *La personnalité humaine dans l'œuvre de Marcel Proust; essai de psychologie littéraire*. Paris: Minard, 1959.

———. "Proust psychologue." *Revue de l'Université-Laval* 9 (1954-55): 421-28.

Zilboorg, G. "The Discovery of the Oedipus Complex (Episodes from Marcel Proust)." *The Psychoanalytic Quarterly* 9 (1939): 279-302.

OHIO UNIVER